CASABLANCA

MOVIES AND MEMORY

MARC AUGÉ

TRANSLATED AND WITH AN

AFTERWORD BY TOM CONLEY

UNIVERSITY OF MINNESOTA PRESS

MINNEAPOLIS · LONDON

The University of Minnesota Press gratefully acknowledges
financial assistance for the translation of this book provided by
the French Ministry of Culture—Centre national du livre.

The first four illustrations in the book, stills from
Casablanca, are printed here courtesy of Photofest.

Originally published in French as *Casablanca;*
copyright Editions du Seuil, 2007.
Published in the collection La Librairie du xxie siècle,
under the direction of Maurice Olender.

Published by the University of Minnesota Press
111 Third Avenue South, Suite 290
Minneapolis, MN 55401-2520
http://www.upress.umn.edu

Library of Congress Cataloging-in-Publication Data
Augé, Marc.
[Casablanca. English]
Casablanca : movies and memory / Marc Augé ;
translated and with an afterword by Tom Conley.
p. cm.
Includes bibliographical references.
ISBN 978-0-8166-5640-0 (hc : alk. paper) —
ISBN 978-0-8166-5641-7 (pb : alk. paper)
1. Casablanca (Motion picture). I. Title.
PN1997.C352A9413 2009
791.43″72—dc22
2009009379

Printed in the United States on acid-free paper

The University of Minnesota is an
equal-opportunity educator and employer.

20 19 18 17 16 15 14 13 12 11 10 09
10 9 8 7 6 5 4 3 2 1

—*I try to remember*
  But I have neither the power nor perhaps the desire.

ROBERT DESNOS, *Oeuvres*

CONTENTS

This text is not an autobiography, but more likely the "montage" of a few memories. I could have chosen other memories—or another montage.

CASABLANCA

Sometimes the idea strikes me that perhaps there is no greater happiness than sitting at the end of the day in the Latin Quarter to see once again an old American movie.

Walking by the Lycée Fénelon, I hasten my pace for fear that the waiting line in front of the Action Christine is already forming. It's never very long, but I want to have my seat in the last row. The woman behind the box-office window, with whom I like to think I share a tacit complicity, usually welcomes me with a happy smile when I stand before the window. The usherette, when I slip a coin into her hand, gratifies me with a "merci," uttered in a personal tone, expressing more than familiarity, a kind of immemorial intimacy. In truth it seems as if I've always known her, even though she is still young, forty at most. The ushers in the movie theaters along the rue des Écoles take part in the same timelessness. Especially the lady of the Champo, whose first duty is to sell tickets but who sometimes leaves her glass cage to gossip with old clients about the weather or passing time.

"Usherettes": since my childhood these sovereign fairies who bear the name *ouvreuse* have opened the doors of an evasion that continues to exert an irresistible attraction upon me, even on morose days when I have the feeling that I myself am surely escaping into the past.

When I was a child my parents (who loved the movies)

took me with them to the Danton because in any event they would never leave me alone at home on a Saturday afternoon. I went to the Danton when I was eight or nine years old. I frequently saw films that were not of my age. My parents exchanged a polite word with the one usherette or the other. At that time, when a new show was about to begin, these *ouvreuses* literally opened the double door at the entry and led you to your seat. On occasion we were late— the documentary had begun—and with a flashlight they illuminated the rows of knees pressed together to pick out three vacant seats side by side. "Pardon me, excuse me please." We snuck through, fearing the release of reproving murmurs. I sat myself as best as I could on the top of the folding seat, which I refused to lower so as to see the screen better. We waited for the documentary and sometimes even a trailer, an attraction, a singer or an illusionist who always inspired in me a sort of compassion because I was becoming well aware that to go on the stage of the Danton between the newsreels and the main feature might not be the sign of a remarkable professional victory.

No, I am not what is called a true cinephile. My memory is lacking; I've seen all the movies, and I can see them over and again without being bored, precisely because I remember them only in rediscovering them. Cinema—I mean the old movies of the Latin Quarter—inspires in me a feeling of "déjà vu" or of having already lived, *déjà vécu* that doubly rekindles my joy because two ordinarily incompatible pleasures get inextricably mixed: anticipation and memory.

A young woman entered. Sveltely tailored and her hair in a bun, she made her effect known. She remained immobile for a few seconds, as if to allow time enough for the male clients who were dispersed about the theater to admire her silhouette. Then she took a few steps forward, her gaze slowly inspecting the different rows, before turning around and walking back to take her seat near the door. The young man plopped in his seat by her side alertly rose and, as if everyone were only awaiting her, the lights began to dim. We were all again about to see *Casablanca.*

. . . . . .

I don't know exactly when I saw *Casablanca* for the first time. The movie was made in 1942. It came out in France in '47. And we didn't wait long to see it. I must have been eleven or twelve years old. In any event, I remember that my parents had guffawed at the way Americans thought of Paris on the eve of the entry of the Germans. Maybe they weren't entirely wrong, but after all we ourselves weren't in Paris at that moment. As soon as he had been mobilized, my father was dispatched to the country and my mother hatched in her head the idea of dashing after him. And, of course, with me. And then I began to realize that no matter what, the hot spots, nightclubs, and jazz joints were completely off my parents' compass. It was another world. All the same they had really enjoyed the film, especially when the "Marseillaise" was struck up in front of the Germans. My father had told me of another "Marseillaise" in another film, in *La grande illusion,* and also of the anthem he and his student friends had sung in the reserve officers' school at Auvours near Le Mans, where they were taking classes when the announcement came of the Germans' imminent arrival. Finally, the Germans had delayed, and so they had time enough to make haste and cross the Loire. Now that was something I knew because I too was there, indeed not really far away, with my mother, who never wanted to be far from her husband and who took pains to follow the tracks of the French army in its retreat.

Everything threw me for a loop in *Casablanca*. Love, chivalric friendship between men. Ingrid Bergman's appearance at the entry of Humphrey Bogart's cabaret. "As Time Goes By," the leitmotif played by Sam, the black pianist. And too, more profoundly—but I had neither the words nor the experience to explain it to myself at the time—the stirring beauty of the body of this woman who seduced men and that observers knew without seeing anything of it (that was the eroticism of the 1940s) that two among them had "had" her.

"As time goes by . . ."

Casablanca was really something else. If the stereotypical exoticism of the streets of the Casbah in the film has always left a strong impression on me, it's because it corresponds to the images that from early childhood the name of this African city had awoken in me, along with a few others with strange sounds, such as Diégo Suarez or Djibouti. All these names punctuated the travels that the great man of the family, my uncle, made to distant lands during the war years. And their unaccustomed consonance added a touch of mystery to the hero and his journey, whose name everyone always spoke to me and whom I would see appear only at the Liberation, with de Gaulle and the Americans. I recall (I am sure of this memory, having verified it on several occasions with my parents) glimpsing my aunt in '39, just when she was about to embark with her two children to catch up with him at Casablanca. At home they spoke to me a lot about Casablanca during the war. They used to say "Casa" in brief, by habit, like the true colonials. Only much later did I begin to understand the complexity of the drama that had been played out in the region in '42, even if they kept speaking in front of me of Noguès, of Giraud, or of Darlan. My uncle, an officer in the navy, never had much knack for politics. Disciplined, he opened fire on the Americans when they disembarked in Morocco. It was only a little later that he became a hero. Opting for the Allies and Free France, he took command of a submarine after a period of training in the United States. At about the same time I noticed that the photograph of Pétain had disappeared from my parents' and my grandparents' homes. My uncle traveled a great deal, to America, to England, to Madagascar. News of him was infrequent and indirect. For a long time they thought he was dead. The Parisian press had announced triumphantly that the German navy had sunk a rebellious submarine. I still see my grandfather in tears returning home to my parents, his newspaper folded under his arm, to deliver the news to them.

I don't know how we ever happened to know the name of the submarine my uncle commanded. When I asked my mother about the subject she was unable to answer. Several years ago, when I began—I'm still not sure why—to press her to speak of the prewar years, of the declaration of war, of the exodus, and of the Occupation, her memories were much clearer. When she reached the age of ninety, I continued exploring this faraway past with her. But I realized that I was suggesting answers to the questions I was posing. I nonetheless pressed on because she also seemed to take pleasure in this exercise.

My uncle wiggled out of the tight squeeze. He never spoke to me of his exploit. But in his place others did. Especially my grandfather, not the least because he was proud of his son and probably too, and more obscurely, because the stunning deed definitely erased the ambiguities of earlier times. The family definitely went over to the good side. My uncle, stopping its engines, had taken the submarine to the bottom of the sea. He released some fuel oil, pretended to be sunk and dead for a few hours, and, as in a number of war movies I've seen since, thus succeeded in fooling enemy patrols before sailing the damaged ship back to harbor.

In '45 he was assigned to the submarine base at La Rochelle. His wife left Casablanca, where she had spent every day of the war with my cousins, to rejoin him. I've sometimes tried to imagine what their reunion might have been like after so many months of adventure and anguish. It was winter. She caught cold. She died, pregnant, of pneumonia, much as in a bad melodrama or a Hemingway novel. If the name "Casablanca" still shines in my eyes with a special aura, it owes a debt to the memory of the dark and handsome hero returning from the war to encounter death, the hero with a tumultuous past, the inconsolable widower with whom women fell headlong in love and who made men crazy with jealousy. I got to know my uncle in the aftermath. He fascinated my adolescence; I saw him grow old. But the image that first comes to mind when I think about him is that of this handsome thirty-five-year-old kid coming right out of history, and whose grief could never smother his desire to live, the desire of this movie hero waiting for a screenplay for which his life would be gloriously fitting. I hardly know Casablanca. I've been through it only on two or three occasions, and rapidly at that. Today the city of my childhood dreams exists only in the Latin Quarter, in Curtiz's film.

Louis Renault and Rick, the Frenchman and the American, had just concluded their friendship pact. I was the last to leave, lost in dreams and even moved as I always am when I see *Casablanca* yet again. I noticed the young and spectacular unknown woman with her hair in a deft bun who was delayed in the hall in front of the piles of blue and pink programs while chattering with her neighbor. He explained to her how the two rooms worked, the one in which the same film is shown for a week or a little more, and the one in which the feature, which changes every day, figures in a thematic program for two or three weeks: gangster movies, westerns, John Ford or Humphrey Bogart . . . "Today," he was commenting, "a Spielberg movie [*Minority Report,* a relatively recent feature] is being shown in the other room for the whole week. In the room we've just exited, next Wednesday you can see Humphrey Bogart in Howard Hawks's *The Big Sleep.* It wasn't part of the Bogart Week but will be chosen for 'The *Noir* Novel on Screen.'" She thanked him for his kindness. He did not visibly displease her. I followed them for a second with my eyes while, continuing their conversation, they walked off toward the rue Saint-André-des-Arts.

Every film we have enjoyed one day takes a place in our memory next to others. Movies are one memory among others, and they submit, like them, to the menace of oblivion, to the erosion of memory. It even happens that for one reason or another, with more or less exactitude, we were recalling the place, the date, and the circumstances when we saw it for the first time. But to remember one film also means remembering film itself, that is, remembering images, somewhat as if the technique of cinema had from the beginning operated the mental labor that selects perceptions in order to turn them into memories, as if in some way it had accomplished the labor of memory. It thus happens that film images swim through our heads like personal memories, as if they were part of our very lives, and moreover with this same degree of incertitude that often affects these memories and is sometimes revealed when we return to the places of our past or from a confrontation with the memories of another. To see a film again, by the same token, can be the occasion for regaining forgotten episodes, but also for measuring the difference between the memory image, which has lived its own life, and that of the screen, that has not changed an iota.

Casablanca is not the oldest film that I recall, because my parents habitually took me to the movies during the war. I seem to recall that when the newsreels—all Vichyist, naturally—were shown, the room sometimes remained lit in order to discourage evil spirits from protesting in favor of obscurity. I can still hear Jules Berry in *Les visiteurs du soir* claiming his sulfurous identity ("the devil" or *diable*) by letting his voice, at once deliciously sardonic and provocative, drag on the "a" of *diable*. Like *Casablanca, Les visiteurs du soir* was made in '42, but Marcel Carné shot it in France. The film was shown in Parisian theaters throughout the Occupation. Censors found nothing to quibble about in this story shaped as a medieval legend, nor with Prévert's dialogue, even if the subtlest or most patriotic spectators had wished to see in the figure of the devil a representation of the German occupier. *Les visiteurs du soir* is surely one of the very first films I saw, maybe even the first, but I really can't be sure.

Times had changed when *Casablanca* came out in France. On every street corner in Paris people were dancing and singing. It was the time of Saint-Granier and of *Ploum ploum tra la la.* For two years I had been running up to American or English soldiers in the streets to beg for sticks of chewing gum or chocolate. *Casablanca* was not my first film, but it was my first experience of time induced by a work of fiction. Not only did the film begin to exist as a memory (a memory of a first time, of an originary, inaugural emotion sustained by a few mythic scenes), but in itself it dealt with memory and remembrance, with fidelity and oblivion; its two heroes were now and again illuminated and tortured by their past. Especially, and for reasons that stuck to my own history—and that caused me as of the age of eleven or twelve to be aware that I had a history—it was, and it remains for me today, a trigger releasing memories. The name alone, "Casablanca," is a font of many evocations and of other names that echo through it. With their properly dramatic order, the periods or the episodes to which the film alludes (the prewar, the exodus, the Occupation) had imposed upon my first years a sense of the past and a taste of the future. The force of the first impressions is such that in the course of my existence I sometimes had the feeling not of reliving the past but of living situations that recalled some of its most particularly intense moments and that even brought them back to life to the degree that they were giving me the sensation of starting life over again, of living a beginning once more. Finally, the essential scenes of the film illustrated insistent, recurring, obsessive themes—waiting, menace, or flight—which by dint of the hazards of history, were imposed upon my childhood, inoculating in me a mixed feeling of exaltation and of slight anguish that always swells up in me on the eve of departure, when I get ready to travel.

Montage: This word, which seems to be borrowed from mechanical engineering, sums up a mystery that brings charm to cinema. How does the linking, one upon the other, of previously selected scenes ever succeed in composing a narrative? For the filmmaker the difficulty of constructing a narrative is greater than what confronts the novelist, who can speak in his or her own proper name, describe, comment, and inform the reader, therefore tell, even if—and perhaps rightly under the influence of cinema —to the contrary he or she can spend time pruning transitions, eradicating dead time ("the marquise went out at five o'clock"), and, opting for a more modern writing, leave to the readers themselves the responsibility of the linkages that form the story. In every event at the cinema we sense well that extraneous words, when oral or written on the screen (voice-over, summaries, diverse indications, commentaries), tend to weaken the image by confining it to a role of illustration.

Such is not the case with the most recent televised American serials that turn the breakneck speed of montage and a brutal editing of scenes into a trademark, indeed, a style of their own. Signs of place, date, and hour are nonetheless written on the screen, but they are at the same time syntactically minimal and narratively essential; through the rapid linking of images the narrative design becomes more legible; they plot its course. They correspond to the disappearance of every transitional image: we are always at the site of action. Their footloose style also influencing many American films, these American serials take to the limit the form of writing that defines cinema in general and causes it to become a profoundly unrealistic art.

Surely in real life bold or decisive moments are rare. They are separated in every event by long periods of time, we easily realize, that have nothing to say for themselves as soon as we try to tell someone what happened to us last night or last week. And still, more often than not, these strong and decisive moments appear before our eyes retrospectively. In general, they are condemned to exist only as memories. In reality, our everyday life is encumbered with little tasks that take time and that we would prefer to be done with—waiting, "traffic jams" of different sorts (and not only those spent in cars): that's what most frequently cinema finesses beginning with the shooting ("Cut!") and, most evidently, in the montage. It spares us the many long minutes of incalculable banality. In the blink of an eye we pass from the moment when the hero sees his buddy die in warfare to when he communes with him over his grave. We leave him in a railway station or at an airport and then barely a few seconds later, we find him at his destination. The movie hero never waits for the subway, never stands in the checkout line at the supermarket, never daydreams in his corner instead of answering his mail. Banal life nestles behind the shortcuts of shooting and in the remainders of the montage.

The hero's life thus defies the laws of gravity that rule the lives of ordinary people, notably the spectators themselves. Even in movies that adopt a slow rhythm, the shortcuts of film writing, that is, of the writing of images, are sensitive. That doesn't mean that cinema is unaware of time. To the contrary, it is obsessed with time. If it leaves the impression of playing with time, it is because the constraints that film imposes (to tell a story in less than two hours) require it to multiply effects of slow motion or of acceleration. Certain dialogues are recorded in real time; therein we can sense hesitations and even the interlocutors' breathing. It happens that the suspense catches our breath as if we were living the moment. Sometimes even the image slows down to convey the subjective feeling of extreme rapidity (when, for example, the filmmaker shoots an automobile accident, as in *The Little Things in Life*). But no sooner than the weightless effect is felt once again are we carried away to another moment and another place. This weightlessness is the same as that of memory that allows us to jump from one past moment to the other by skimming over details and transitions. But when cinema invites us to reach back into the past of its characters, its flashbacks are not those of memory: they conjugate the past in the present. The story of the past takes place in the present. Such is the force of the image: imposing itself upon us, it always brings us back to the present of the action. When the director wants to embrace the subjectivity of one of the characters of the movie, say, in recalling a childhood memory, he or she must go back to written text that an actor reads in voice-over, in a tone of confidence or nostalgia, or even eventually shuffle the image by playing on its tone to make for the time being a sort of metaphor of the text.

The effect of weightlessness for the most part results from montage. After a day of shooting, the rushes in themselves do not constitute a story. They await being cut and concatenated. A director's personality can moreover be measured beforehand by the liberty he or she takes with the screenplay (when he or she is not its author) and afterward by the liberty taken (or not taken) with the film editor. During the shooting of *Casablanca* it seems that Curtiz, to the confusion of the players, had no clear idea of how the story would develop and conclude. It was built from day to day, scene by scene, by dint of inspiration. Surely this form of improvisation is relatively rare, but it tells us something about the relation of movies to memory. Faced with his rushes, the director somewhat resembles an aging man who tries, as they say, to "pull his memories together." When we don't have a very good memory (one that records, that dates, and that classifies), the past—even the relatively immediate past—most often comes to us as an array of dispersed "scenes." At the moment of remembrance we try to retrieve the bond that unites them, the thread that runs from the one to the other, the very thread of existence. The double paradox of memory is that as the past becomes increasingly remote, the more the scenes that remain in our minds appear vivid, colored, and present; but, on the contrary, the more the thread that binds them becomes tenuous, the more confused or lost it gets. We need to "mount" or "make a montage" of our memories, these rushes of memory, in order to recompose a continuity, to turn it into a story. What plays out in this operation is hardly for naught, since losing one's past (progressively and tragically, as in Alzheimer's disease, the most remote memories that disappear after a last resistance) means losing sight of oneself, in other words, dying.

The exodus marked my childhood. I was four and a half when my mother took me on the roads of France in pursuit of my father. In what followed quite often the departures for summers in Brittany gave me the feeling of beginning the exodus all over again, if only because we always went through the villages and cities that had dotted our itinerary. For me the Loire River has always been a border.

As soon I set off on the road west I have the vague impression of fleeing. Among other reasons, that explains why I love an actor like Trintignant: When he was younger he was always fleeing in his movies. He always went at a gallop, taking off as if death were hot on his heels. And for me too, every other night in my dreams I'm in flight, I'm running at full tilt. In my dreams my legs are still in great shape. From the exodus I still have a map of France from which memory recalls a few notable points (Champagné, Le Mans, Bordeaux, Canéjan, Tarbes, Caylus, Toulouse, Brive) without really tying them together chronologically. I don't know why I had to wait until 2000 to experience the desire to retrieve and, while chatting with my mother, to follow once again every stage of this itinerary. In fact, it was in my memories where I sought to assign some order. They were laden with images having no immediate relation with each other and, besides, I suspected that some of them, strictly speaking, happened slightly before or after the exodus. I had needed my mother to follow the thread, through the labyrinth of our common wandering, that would bring me back to my starting point, to Paris of the prewar years or of the time before the exodus.

The starting point is my grandparents' place on the quai de la Tournelle. There I see my aunt and her two children in '39, before they left for Casablanca. In a way they gave the signal to depart, but we remained unaware. My grandparents also left before the Germans arrived and soon found sanctuary in Corrèze at the home of the owners of the garage that my grandfather used to manage. Upon their return the garage was closed. They then moved. Up to 1940 they had an apartment in a vast dilapidated structure (I can still see the long corridor with chipped tiles on which I pulled my little red wooden fire truck) from which the Seine and Notre-Dame were visible. When I go by the lofty portal of this eighteenth-century private dwelling that today is entirely restored and divided into five or six upscale apartments, I am sometimes taken by the desire to knock and enter. But a modern portal, whether of the time or having the same appearance, can't be opened just like that. The door code and the surveillance camera have always discouraged me from giving way to my desire.

Certain images are more tenacious than others. In my eyes the exodus is first of all a stay in a village called Champagné a few kilometers from Le Mans. A military camp that I suppose still exists—the Auvours camp—adjoined this village. There my father spent some time as a student in the reserve officer training corps, the EOR. The names Champagné and Auvours, along with the mysterious acronym EOR (which was pronounced in a single breath as if it were magical formula), have always summed up in my mind the beginning of the exodus, this brief period that preceded our escapade along the roads of France. There is another name: the Golden Pheasant, which was a restaurant where we took our meals. A distinguished lady with blond hair and wearing a gray suit ate at the table next to ours. I found her attractive. She fascinated me. I, who have no memory for names, always turned around to look at her. My mother was stupefied, and I even more so, when she suddenly heard me say, as we were recalling the days spent in Champagné, the Golden Pheasant, and our neighbor lady in the dining room, "She was called Madame Pichon!" More than sixty years had passed and all of a sudden this name unconsciously passed my lips. Up to the time it sprang forth I was unaware that it had been concealed in a cranny of my memory. By the same token, I haven't the slightest memory of the hotel where we used to sleep and where, now and again, my father came to join my mother after having fled his dormitory with the complicity of his friends. Later they spoke with me while joking about these moments of furtive happiness, their last memory of youth, I sometimes said to myself, because a year later my father was struck by an illness that caused him to age prematurely.

In Champagné some relatively peaceful days flowed by, but surely they were few. My mother had just met another young woman who also had shadowed her husband as far as Champagné. We went for walks in the neighboring pine forests. All that went on at the very same moment in the movie when Rick and Ilsa were drinking their last bottle of champagne while listening to Sam play "As Time Goes By." The summer was hot. We often gathered wild strawberries. One day my mother held me back just when I was going to put my hand on a viper, hidden in the thick of the tendrils, that raised its head before slithering away. My mother's cry terrified me. I also was terrified a little later by the *vroom* of a German airplane flying just over the pine trees and on whose wing a black cross was visible. We often recalled these two episodes. The images I still have of them are vivid and, it seems for a long time now, remain intact. Another image joins them: it is night; we are in our new friend's car. We've left Champagné. My mother uses a flashlight to illuminate the road because the headlights don't work or perhaps we've been asked to extinguish them. I can't recall exactly. A policeman leans through the lowered car window.

I'm snuggled up in the back. He explains that we can't continue on the way to Rennes because the Germans are already there. He advises the lady driving to go instead toward the Loire.

Before my mother helped me bring order to my memories, I took "my" exodus to be a long circular evasion going west, then south, followed by the armistice and the return to Paris. The story that I might have made of it was simple. After the episode with the policeman, we had driven, I seem to recall, for a long time. I slept a lot and awoke in the home of our older lady friend in Basque country: from the window of the bedroom I could see the Pyrenees. This vision is still before my eyes: the summits are snowcapped (at least in my vision). Later we looked all around for my father, from Tarbes to Toulouse. I can see a large square and a huge barracks at whose door stands guard a black soldier with a red fez. But it was at Caylus that we found him. The image from Caylus that I recall is one of soldiers busy slitting the throats of pigs: pigs wail like babies and their blood flows into the street. The story has to end somewhere around there because in the next shot I am with my parents and my father is dressed in civilian clothes. We are at Brive, in the clinic where my grandfather has just been operated on for a stomach ulcer. My father takes me into his arms so that I can wave to him from the other side of the glass door.

The following image is that of the place Maubert, where, at the exit of the metro, I glimpse my first German soldier in a gray uniform. In this version there were a few images that I couldn't quite pigeonhole: the lower house of my maternal great-grandmother, in the Landes, at Canéjan, not far from Bordeaux; I can hear the cowbells tinkling as night falls. I saw the house a few years after the death of my great-grandmother, but the herd of cows on the Landes pastures had vanished. Coming back to me too, and frequently, is a glimpse of La Rochelle (of the arcades all along a wide street), most likely before the exodus.

With delicate touches, digging around in her memories, my mother helped me complete and rectify this scenario. We didn't succeed immediately because our conversations were chaotic and went somewhat in every direction, one memory calling forth another and opening parentheses that we often forgot to close. The story that we finally settled upon relates a series of events at once important and derisory. I believe I recall certain of them quite clearly. Others have disappeared forever from my memory, but my mother helped me specify a few scattered images and put them into place.

So it was in August 1939 that we were on vacation at Châtelaillon, near La Rochelle; there we spent part of the month of August. War was declared on September 3 (on its eve I was four years old). My father had been billeted to

Paris but advised my mother to stay in La Rochelle and
to wait and see what would happen. A little before Christmas, because nothing had happened, we returned to Paris.
In April 1940 my father was mobilized and assigned to
Tarbes. My mother nonetheless decided to follow him.
She took me with her in a train to Bordeaux, where we
stopped to spend a day in Canéjan with my great-grandmother. We had to take a tram from Bordeaux, then walk
for a good stretch on the Landes moor before we reached
the village nestled in the pines some kilometers off the main
road. We had scarcely arrived in Tarbes before we had to
pull up and leave. My father had just been assigned to the
Auvours camp. We went back through Bordeaux, went
once again to say hello to the grandmother, and took the
train to Le Mans. From there a local bus delivered us to
Champagné the same day. We caught sight of the camp,
my mother was able to regain contact with my father, and
then we returned. In the night an alert sounded. A few
planes flew over the city (I have no memory of them). The
next day we took the local bus once again and set forth to
move to Champagné. In the hotel my mother became ac-
quainted with the woman who was going to pilot us in what
soon become our exodus. We witnessed the arrival of a
crowd of refugees; my mother recalled that there were
many Belgians among them. When it seems as if I now retain a few images from the montage, I can't be sure if I'm

not confusing them with shots from *Forbidden Games*. When we fled Champagné in the car of our new friend, Madame Inchauspé, and in the company of two other women (I forgot them, too, and I still can't recall them), it was first of all with the idea of leaving her in Rennes and of our taking refuge with my father's family farther off in Brittany. But in La Guerche-de-Bretagne, where the firemen gave us a little gasoline, we were informed that the road to Rennes was blocked. A little later we were strafed by some planes, probably Italian. This incident left a deep impression on my mother, but I haven't the slightest memory of it. We then went on to Bordeaux via the Vendée and once again found ourselves with my great-grandmother in Canéjan. The following night Bordeaux, where a certain number of French leaders were going to embark upon the *Massilia*, was bombed. From our refuge in the Landes we could hear the bombardment, my mother said, but I haven't retained the slightest inkling of it, as if whatever struck great fear in me has been eliminated from my conscience. The next day we took off for the Pyrenees. Two days later we boarded the train for Toulouse, where my mother believed she could find her husband. She inquired at several barracks before finally learning that he was stationed at Caylus, where we met him when we arrived by way of Montauban. There she rented a room where in the morning we were awoken by the cries of pigs being slaughtered in the street. The rest roughly corresponds to my memories. We reached my grandparents in Brive. From there we took the train to Paris and crossed the line of demarcation in the middle of the night. We arrived at the Austerlitz station. My mother did not recall the German soldier in the gray uniform whom I see over and over again, at the moment of our arrival at the place Maubert.

Thus as years passed by I had reduced our complex itinerary to a few essential scenes, encumbered with detours and returns, that my mother had improvised during our wandering in France. But why were these scenes so essential to me? Even a long psychoanalysis would in most instances be unable to answer this question completely. I simply note that they all correspond to pauses in movement, to the days after arrival that were also the eves of departure, to moments of waiting, of anticipation and of "suspense" inasmuch as the latter designates at once the suspension of time and the imminence of the event. In the flat countryside of Champagné, just as in that of Canéjan, in the stopped car from whose backseat I heard the voice of the policeman who forbade us to go ahead, I was fully living an instant, as intense as it was ephemeral, that relentlessly kept me on the edge of the future.

．　．　．　．　．　．

Why is Rick (Humphrey Bogart) so bitter, so hard-boiled at the beginning of the film? Why does he leave us with the impression of having *returned from everything and all*? Because he has a history that he can't swallow: he was tricked, betrayed by Ilsa (Ingrid Bergman), the woman of his dreams, the woman with a limpid gaze and a suffusing voice; it's because he was made from movies that he told stories to himself. On the one side an illusion and on the other a lie: such his history, such his story. When he meets Ilsa again in Casablanca he doesn't want to listen to her, to hear the other story, her own story. He wants no part of it, just as for months he refuses to listen to the refrain of "As Time Goes By" that would open his wound. And then, all of a sudden, the roles turn topsy-turvy. Ilsa looked stunning at the beginning of the film. She had suffered, but for a good cause. She could tell herself an honorable story, the one that she cannot convince Rick to hear when they meet again: her husband, a hero of the Resistance, whom she took for dead and who has returned, this past that she had never told to her lover and who has surfaced at the last second, impeding her from fleeing with Rick. Her dilemma is that Rick is converted when he hears this honorable story of resistance and sacrifice, and he even wants to add a new chapter at the very moment when she herself is ready to renounce it in order finally to plunge once again into her love story. The end of *Casablanca* is thus this decisive and ambiguous moment in which the two protagonists cast the memory of their love in an enduring shape. Only a few months separate their passionate romance in Paris from their new encounter in Casablanca. Their confusion (which the spectator immediately discerns) is also that of the actors (Ingrid Bergman had asked Curtiz which of the two men she would eventually love) and of the director (Curtiz answered: "Play it between the two"). Had Curtiz been Corneille, Ilsa, like Bérénice in *Tite et Bérénice,* would have declaimed heroically:

> C'est à force d'amour que je m'arrache au vôtre
> Et je serais à vous si j'aimais comme une autre.

> [Because of my love I tear myself from yours
> And I would be yours had I loved as another.]

Curtiz clearly leans in the direction of a more Racinian Ilsa ("Dans un mois, dans un an . . ." [In a month, in a year . . .]). And in Rick he invests something of Titus's bad faith in *Bérénice.* Rick is the one who ultimately cuts the knot, readily sacrificing love for the sake of honor and the war. Perhaps we need to realize that men decidedly love war and that they are more vainglorious than amorous: Rick handles his chivalric gesture with greater ease as soon as he is certain that he is still loved. Like Musset's Margot, however, we cannot hold back our tears at the spectacle of the melodrama. It is because of the faces, first of all, those moved and moving faces in close-ups whose slightest nuances we decipher as if they were our own destiny. Because of this slight *floating effect,* the characters' attitudes, owed perhaps to the director's hesitations, underscore the uncertainties of life, of our illusions and of our disillusions— those of memory, soon, as if the uncertainties of remembrance, by some sort of strange fidelity, were reproducing those of the past. It is because of this need for sadness and for beauty that we happen to feel in the lofty places of distress and separation, in railway stations, at airports, that now and then a refrain will surge forward unconsciously. It's because we need to believe in love, in heroism, and in self-denial that we instinctively adhere to the most romantic version of the story and, in the secrecy of our memory, give way to the intimate and personal montage of our film, this film whose title, *Casablanca,* flickers every time we pronounce it, that hereafter resonates in us as if it were a memory coming out of a distant past.

Two or three years ago, some hours of insomnia became the occasion for a special kind of investigation. I threw myself headlong into the recovery of my earliest memories, those before 1940. In the night I amassed shards of images that I couldn't shake out of my head and, when the day came, I ran to my mother to encourage her to talk and to try to establish with her a few cross-checks that would allow me to date them. She was an essential witness in this enterprise, but her memory was weakening or rather drifting away, and it was exploring only those areas of which I myself had no experience. For she too was going back to beginnings and was more eagerly recalling the twenties, indeed the end of the First World War, than the years 1937 or '38. She spoke to me of the house of her childhood in Amiens or of her father's friends as if I had known them, and excused herself for her absentmindedness when I protested, with a small laugh that won me a little indulgence: "Oh! That's true, you hadn't yet been born . . ." I understood well that the worst solitude was that of memories, and that my mother was suffering because those who had borne witness to what she had lived were gone. But I put her back on track somewhat harshly when she threatened to go on a tangent, no doubt for fear of losing her, of myself remaining alone with my memories.

▪

I have an exact memory that I really can't confirm whether it goes back to '38 or '39. An elegant apartment in the seventh arrondissement, toward Ségur or Duroc, occupied by one of my grandmother's sister, quite naturally, who had married an artillery officer from a well-to-do family. She took in her daughter, who, likewise married to a military man and already the mother of three, was preparing to join her husband in Algeria. They had offered me (maybe it was for my birthday, in which case I was just three years old) a toy tank, equipped with treads, that spit fire while inching over picture books that we placed in front of it to impede its advance. My family—with the exception of my grandfather, who nonetheless had known a few of the years before and after the Great War, and of my father, discharged in his youth, who had all the same been mobilized in 1940—was composed of men with military careers. From '39 up to Dien Bien Phu, in my eyes these men endlessly transformed the history of France into a sort of family history. That being said, in my generation I am the oldest boy and while I am almost the only one not to have had a career in the military, I am also the only one to have known the Algerian War. By way of a paradox whose irony I once savored, but whose currency is lost today from the standpoint of my first and second cousins, all professional warriors who more or less specialized in humanitarian service, it was I, the so-called egghead, the presumed subversive, who for some time had figured as a former combatant.

On Sundays before the war we often met at the Parc Saint-Maur. We took the train from the Bastille station, where the Opera is now situated. We used to go to the home of one of my grandmother's sisters; she was by far the richest member of the family and lived in an imposing house surrounded by a park that seemed to me to be absolutely immense. For me the Parc Saint-Maur was my great-aunt's park. A few photos that my parents kept and that we used to look at from time to time have endlessly inspired memories of the house and the lawns of the garden. But only two images remain really present up to now. The first is that of the bathroom, where I thought I was being smothered under a jet of water from a shower that the housekeeper made me take. This first accession to domestic modernity (my parents used to wash me in a basin) panicked me and probably since has inspired in me a fear of water that I've never been able to overcome completely. The second is that of the Peugeot and the garage in the corner of a park that sheltered it—the odor of gasoline in the garage was agreeably heady, but that of the car when the door was half-opened, hot and sickeningly sweet, made me nauseated. I've also retained the vague memory of a slow and prudent walk (no one seemed to have complete confidence in my great-aunt, who was learning how to drive) along the shores of the Marne. All these impressions reach back to the beginning of 1939 or, maybe, to '38.

Before '39 everything is confused. There remain three names, an odor, and an image. Before the war my parents had taken their vacations at Châtelaillon, on the Atlantic seashore, and at Lion-sur-Mer, on the English Channel. On one of these beaches they were selling . . . I can't quite remember: marshmallows or caramelized pralines, some sweets with a very sugary odor that, I'm sure if I were to retrieve it, would restore an entire panel of my first childhood; but I've never entirely recovered it and, with each effort I've made to try to find it (when in a pastry shop or at a county fair), like a forgotten word on the tip of my tongue, it fled my grasp and sank deeper in the shoals and folds of my memory. A frustrated Proustian, I console myself in saying that a change of recipe and of aroma is perhaps the origin of my disillusion. A third name, Chantilly, always enchanted me in childhood by its sweetness and by everything it suggested, countryside and cream, forest and flowers, but still more because of the anecdote attached to it and of which over the years they never hesitated to remind me. My grandfather drove a little Citroën, one of these cranky convertibles that can still be seen in parades of collectors of old cars.

One Sunday my grandparents took me for a drive. They stopped for a moment in the direction of Chantilly and, when they talked about resuming the trip, I made a scene by demanding to take the steering wheel. That could only have happened during the summer of '38, when I thus wasn't even three. The episode was recounted to me so often over time that I've probably embellished the memory. But there is one thing for sure that I could not have invented: the rapture into which I was suddenly plunged at the sight of endless poppies from the roadside where the car was parked. The spectacle inspired my first aesthetic emotion: dazzling colors, blazing light, and perpetual movement because the poppies, light flowers quivering in the breeze that was making the fields ripple, awakened in me ideas of departure that will never be gone and for which my impetuous desire to take the wheel was surely a first expression. When at the age of eighteen I began to read the passage in *In Search of Lost Time* in which the sight of a poppy lost on an embankment below a wheat field inspires in the traveler an emotion analogous to what would make him exclaim, when he suddenly glimpses a boat lying high and dry at some distance from the shore,

"The sea!" It instantly awoke in me the luminous image of this edge of the road in the Île-de-France, where for the first time I felt the urgent need to go off and away.

A few months ago (but I've given it up because no one now can guide me in this play of uncertain itineraries), I loved to embark thus every night in search of the point beyond which I would feel my conscience ravished for having ever existed. This slow climb back into time resembled something of an adventure, an expedition always destined for naught, but always begun over and again, not toward the source of the Nile or the of the Amazon, but toward the other frontier, death.

When I went to say hello to my mother on that evening, she seemed almost not to have strength enough to raise her gaze toward me, as if it were too heavy, too laden with bitterness. She made it look affected, surely, to underline, without saying so, that over the past five or six days I'd made myself scarce. Fortunately, I knew a good remedy: no sooner had I promised to have lunch with her the next day than a smile illuminated her face. She had found her wit and drive as if by magic and took up where we left off in the conversation of the week before: "I've reflected on what you asked. In '37 we were living in Poitiers, and we spent our vacation in Châtelaillon. We went back to Châtelaillon in '39, in the month of August, just before the declaration of war. And so Lion-sur-Mer was during the summer of '38."

And I suddenly felt happy, I can't say why, for having been able to date one of my first memories with a degree of certitude. Memory is moreover not truly the word: this trace, rather, of a sensation that had formerly brushed alongside before I took refuge in this name, Lion-sur-Mer, that still floats in my memory like a balloon at a local carnival released by the clumsy hand of an unknown child, himself having vanished in the night of time.

. . . . . .

What I love in old films, especially old American films, are less the films (even if many are excellent) than the actors. On each occasion I find them unchanged, handsome as gods and goddesses, or, in every instance, expressive, powerful, embodying virtue or evil, courage or cowardice (more often virtue and courage, to be sure). They haven't acquired a wrinkle. They remain faithful to the first image they gave of themselves when we were young. James Stewart and Kim Novak, Humphrey Bogart and Lauren Bacall, Ingrid Bergman, John Wayne and Maureen O'Hara, Robert Mitchum and Marilyn, Montgomery Clift, Clark Gable and Vivien Leigh, Spencer Tracy and Katharine Hepburn, Elizabeth Taylor and Richard Burton, Henry Fonda, Richard Widmark, Gene Tierney, Rita Hayworth, Orson Welles, Errol Flynn, Burt Lancaster, Cary Grant, Barbara Stanwyck, Gary Cooper, Kirk Douglas, Glenn Ford, Edward G. Robinson, Newman and Redford, Gene Kelly and Cyd Charisse, Fred Astaire and Ginger Rogers, and so many others, and also all those supporting roles (Walter Brennan . . .) and all the admirable film noir of B vintage: an eternal fountain of youth.

When I'm at the movies, the characters I see on the screen are large, larger than me, just as adults were when I was a child. The movies give us a child's vision. If I prefer not to watch videocassettes or DVDs, it is first of all for reasons of proportion. When the narrator of *In Search of Lost Time* returns to the places of his childhood, next to his memories he finds them small and shriveled. Movies are less deceiving. Certainly the adults who go to the movies have grown, but the seated spectators' position puts them almost at the same level as the children they were. In front of the big screen, they can without risk test the fidelity of their gaze in retrieving the immutable images of a film discovered years before.

When I reflect on my parents, on my grandparents, or on other members of my family who now have vanished, the first image that comes to mind is one of youth, I mean of my youth, and, as a consequence, of theirs too, at least relatively: my grandfather at sixty or sixty-five, my father and my mother at thirty or thirty-five. I've sometimes dreamed of my father, but rarely. On each occasion he comes forward natural, youthful, and kindly, as if we had never left one another, as if I had never aged, as if we had never had an argument; he was there in all eternity, even if another part of me, even inside of the dream, knew that I was dreaming. He had the beauty of memory and of movies. I have other images, of course—images of sickness, of old age, and of death—but it's almost always the image of youth that is the first to return.

The miracle of cinema is that I don't imagine this image, I see it. One evening two or three years ago a documentary about Audrey Hepburn was being shown on television. Gregory Peck, who was still in fairly sharp form, a full head of white hair and still with black eyebrows, was explaining why she was so charming. The documentary was a little dated. Gregory Peck had already been dead for some time. It was somewhat strange to see the image of this dead man, still alive, who was speaking of an already dead woman—as if he had become her younger brother. But a few minutes later, in recalling *Roman Holiday,* you were also forgetting the old Gregory and the exhausted face of Audrey in illness. There they were, the two of them, fresh and alive, not like a faithful recollection, but a piece of the past encrusted in the present! A past present, with its own past and its own future. Another temporality was taking control of you and, from the beginning, irresistibly: that of the story that you know by heart, but which recaptivated you nonetheless and didn't let you go until the last scene—when the two Corneillian heroes resigned to their fate conscientiously do their best to turn their fleeting present into a memory.

In the eyes of those who see the film again after a

number of years, it is a sort of long flashback. To see a film again is to recover a past that retains all the vivacity of the present.

Actors age. Sometimes brilliantly: the Marlon Brando of *The Godfather* or of *Apocalypse Now* has little to do with the Brando of *Viva Zapata!* But neither of the characters fashioned from these two Marlon Brandos detracts from the other. There probably exist a number of detailed studies of actors' careers. It can be estimated that among them one or another has aged well or aged badly; that he or she may or may not have found age-appropriate roles. On television we see countless documentaries that recount the "legends" of the most prestigious actors, of their lives, their loves, and their last days. But spectators who watch a movie are generally plunged into the temporality that the film imposes; both plot and characters are intertwined. Actors age with impunity because they are always the age of their role. Characters, by contrast, don't change, and the few female stars who, following the example of Greta Garbo, no longer worked after reaching a certain age were dead wrong if they thought they thus were preserving the image spectators had of them. This image is not that of the star but that of the roles she played. Each role is autonomous and evades the law of time.

The miracle of the movies is that they impose the physical evidence of the heroes who retain their youth while we grow older. They are never younger than when the actors who embodied them are dead and have thus become what a few of them had always dreamed of being: characters definitely withdrawn from the erosion of biological time. But this preserved youth in no way inspires in us any nostalgia. It preserves our own; it resuscitates immutable images and delivers to us the proof that we have existed even while the conscience of passing time would rather impose on us evidence of the inverse: the sensation of our decomposing as time passes by in order soon to vanish, to be nothing more than a shard of memory that will float for still a little more time in the memory of our elders before sinking with them into oblivion.

Once or twice I was somewhat curt in interrupting my mother while, in a moment of fatigue, somewhat lost in the images of her past, she let herself recall an episode prior to my birth as if we had lived it together. "But you're talking about my father, about your husband. Come on now, Maman, think again!" "That's true," she uttered after a second of silence and without showing any sign of confusion. But I had the feeling that my father was dying a second time and that I had definitely taken his place. This substitution of identity bothered me less for its phantasms of incest—

because the time was over for me to finish killing my father: the last time I killed my poor father was a few years ago, when I reached and then passed his age at the time of his death. It was then I became his older brother—because my mother was sending me back beyond the time of my birth, in the void in which she was imagining herself perceiving me, a shadow confused with that of my dead father, a ghost before its time, a child stillborn.

The source of *Casablanca* is a stage play no one talks about anymore. Cinema has adapted every literary genre: epics, tales, stories from antiquity, the Bible, Shakespeare, and the entire romantic canon in all of its diversity, from Stendhal to Tolstoy, from Alexandre Dumas to Thomas Mann, from Victor Hugo to Hemingway or Pasternak. For all that, cinema is not basically an art of adaptation. Many of its great works are original. Furthermore, some specific cinematic genres have been born. If some whodunit novels or theatrical comedies have been adapted to the screen, the gangster film and the musical comedy are real genres that original creations have illustrated. And as for the "western," well, it has practically never had recourse to adaptation.

To specify what constitutes the essence of the seventh art, we would need to add that if all literary and dramatic genres can be seen on the silver screen, the inverse is not true. Cinema captures all existing narrative modes but never lets anything take off from itself. No theatrical play, no novel has ever been inspired by a film. Recently a few short-lived attempts have been made to market "novels" composed from screenplays, but this subgenre of literature has not witnessed any success.

Cinema is thus this oceanic universe into which all literary currents happen to be thrown without hope of return. It's also the most popular art, the art that imposes upon millions of spectators the images and the faces of its heroes and heroines, and to the very point of replacing the traits of its actors with those that the readers of novels imagine deep down inside themselves. In all probability it is difficult today to reread *Death in Venice* without thinking of Dirk Bogarde or *For Whom the Bell Tolls* without seeing Ingrid Bergman and Gary Cooper.

What, then, is the secret of the seventh art? What allows it to attract to itself the most diverse forms of expression without ever being taken over by any of them? What is the secret of its *force of attraction*?

This secret ought to be sought, I believe, along the lines of the particular aptitude that cinema has in figuring solitude—figuring solitude, in other words, simultaneously to personify and to stage it too. Cinema is an art of solitude, not because some of its major works have as their principal character a solitary individual, but because all its technical resources concur in "figuring solitude."

A film is a combination of three gazes: that of the camera, which obeys the director; that of the principal character, with whom it happens that the camera identifies when the lens becomes "subjective"; and that of the spectator, whom the other two take in hand for the duration of the film's projection. Paradoxically, it is this last gaze, the gaze of the spectator, however subject to the other two, that makes or undoes the film according to how it is or is not guided by the former and is or is not identified with the latter.

In the great majority of films the hero is almost always constantly present. Spectators rarely ever let the character disappear from view. Their identification with the character goes through an effect of recognition that in no way implies any cognition, be it real or imaginary. This recognition is immediate. Of a generous nature, it is generally accorded to the character and is even eventually nourished by the mystery that bears on his or her past.

Cinematic identification is different from that which operates when we read a novel. In the movies the image precedes the stage of identification. And it is the image of a real body; it has none of the blur of a mental image that, however insistent or charged it may be, has gone through the double filter of writing and reading. We need to admit, furthermore, that a movie spectator identifies less with characters than with situations; the entire art of cinema entails staging those situations that have in common the fact of being at once spatial and temporal, as in the cases of exemplary figures, along with their respective variants, that are flight and return, or yet again, departure and arrival. Each of these situations is illustrated by turns in medium shots and close-ups (closing in on a face, an expression, a gaze) and by long shots, a progressive or sudden distancing that reduces the body to a silhouette. This alternation does not proceed without reminding spectators of the relation that holds them with its own images, even when they inquire of their own past in order to obtain a sense of their present moment.

The rereading of a novel after an interval of a few years can become the occasion for different impressions and interpretations. The reader is always to an extent the author of the novel he or she reads or rereads. In theater the same play is habitually restaged and with different actors: another interpretation of the play and, eventually of its characters, is thus proposed to the spectators. Nothing of that order pertains in the movies (unless I put aside "remakes"): it is always the same movie that the lover of film rediscovers, including the same characters and the same actors. If the film that the spectator sees seems to have "aged" (as they say), it's the connoisseur who in fact has changed. The person no longer has the same taste or the same freshness; perhaps, too, time and experience have sharpened his or her critical acuity. But actors have nothing to do with a spectator's feeling of disappointment. The cause is solely in the screenplay, the staging, or the general theme. Two solitudes thus are made manifest in the movie theater: this spectator, who has changed, takes leave of the one that he or she was formerly, when the person saw the film for the first time and when all that remains is to leave the character, who has lost all force of attraction or fascination, to his fate. But it does not exclude finding the actor in another role and in another film.

If *Casablanca* risks having reached a certain age, despite all its inaccuracies and improbable turns, it's because the mythic scenes of departure and arrival abound and engender one another. Ilsa's arrival in Casablanca, Rick's return, the flashback to Paris, the wait in the railway station, the obsession with departure, the haunting fear of separation, the night at the airport, America and Brazzaville on the horizon of the woman in love and of the recovered combatant; the alternation of faces in close-ups and silhouettes fading into the chiaroscuro of the screen; the alternation of the fleeting past and the future taking place, from "As Time Goes By" and the "Marseillaise": all are scenes that we ceaselessly reinvent in our imagination and that for this reason continue to surprise us as we see them over and again.

Cinema must remain the occasion of a meeting or encounter. That is the other reason why I am not a lover of DVDs. To have a film in one's hand, like a book from a library, is tantamount to eradicating the chance of a meeting, or creating an excessive familiarity, of running the risk of repetition and of saturation. When the melody turns into a repeated refrain, all at once are lost the charm of the past and the desire of the future that drive the intensity of the present.

Like those of tragedy, movie heroes need witnesses. The supporting roles in the movies, the confidants of classical tragedy, or the chorus of Greek tragedy punctuate the protagonists' movements with sidelong glances, a few words or various silences that amount to as many commentaries. Everyone is at once an actor and a spectator, a spectator present onstage or on-screen.

In westerns or war movies, the task of the supporting roles is notably to calm the atmosphere with a joke or a cynical remark. In an ambience of anguish they thus gain a distance with respect to the event while underscoring its ineluctable character, in front of which all individual will, however fierce it may be, is shown to be powerless. They are then related to the chorus of classical tragedy, like the silent and pusillanimous crowds that in the most tragic westerns follow the protagonists to the final duel and remain at a respectable distance. Sometimes a woman is the hapless witness of destiny, as when, in *Last Train from Gun Hill,* she loves both of the men who face each other in mortal combat.

In comedy or melodrama the supporting role more often serves as witness to the love affairs of the two principal characters. It is not true that lovers are alone in the world. They need the gaze of another (the best friend, the boss, or the bartender) who proves to them that they exist, that the present exists. This testimony becomes all the more necessary as their love is increasingly fragile or threatened.

The supporting role is fashioned for the passive witness of destiny and the active instrument of the story. For the story stages this character's point of view, and it is most often through him or her that we gain access to the few details around which the drama is tied and the narrative is constructed.

In *Casablanca* Sam has an exemplary supporting role. He utters few words (except when he sings). An African American of the 1940s, he follows his boss wherever he goes, but he is not his interlocutor. He simply has seen all, heard all, understood all; and his talent as pianist grants him the power to revivify the past. "Play it, Sam!": when Sam, transgressing Rick's interdiction, yields to Ilsa's request and replays "As Time Goes By," he sends them back to the story they share. And so it must be told. Sam and his melody interpret the instant of the flashback (this past conjugated in the present).

Sam is solitude itself. He disappears at the moment his boss decides to reshape his life. Fortunately Rick, a manager on the political left, took care to find him another employer. But when Rick changes his life, he also changes companions and leaves with his new friend and fellow combatant. Sam was merely the witness of a moment, and, once the moment is past, nothing remains to which he can or must bear witness.

Sam's disappearance betrays his solitude and, indirectly, that of the former lovers for whom he no longer needs to attest. But Sam also personifies the essential solitude of all those who, engaged in a story that needed them for a certain time, find themselves adrift as soon as it is over or is transformed. Former combatants in bygone wars, retired adventurers, survivors of many shipwrecks, of fleeting loves or disillusioned friendships—one day or another we all share the feeling that life could have been different but that it continues. According to the mood of the day, we feel ourselves being either very free or very alone.

Nothing contrasts more than the opposition of black and white. In the movies, black and white is a source of light. Every film in black and white has its own dominant tonality that casts into infinite nuances. When Rick goes into his room and turns on a light he discovers Ilsa, standing before the window, looking at Casablanca by night. She turns toward him, her face still in shadows, and we see her from Rick's point of view. Neither he nor we can ever forget this apparition. For him, for us too, unreal, and standing before our eyes, she is already a memory.

. . . . . .

When an individual's story crosses through history as such, on the occasion of a more or less dramatic event (a war, a general strike, a revolution . . .), he or she begins to live more attentively: every minute counts, signs are everywhere, nothing is negligible. Hence the paradox of these moments of fear or of hope: they eliminate the morose tenor of everyday life; they disperse depression; and, later, once the menaces or the promises they seem to have borne have vanished, they become indelibly written in memory. They inspire in those who have lived them an immense nostalgia—as if a present pregnant with the future were first of all the promise of a memory.

The charm of *Casablanca* for those who lived the moment that this film portrays holds to this very clash of temporal dimensions. The film is shot in 1942. The episode it relates can only take place in '41. The waiting and anticipations of the characters are the same as those of the director and the producers of the film. In '42 the Americans disembark at Casablanca—despite my uncle's brief and symbolic resistance! When the film arrives in France, in '47, it has already acquired an aged and mythic look, yet it still shimmers with history.

I don't always spend my time thinking about movies and about *Casablanca,* but today, when I recall the various peripatetics of my existence, without really knowing why they continue to occupy my mind, I sometimes happen to associate the film with emotions, faces, and landscapes that, although they belong to fiction, survive in me as memories.

A mellowing of atmosphere: great chunks of remembrance fall away from my memory and float adrift on the currents that carry them off. I watch them as they pass by. Alternatively I draw my gaze on the baroque form of one, the subtle colors of another, the transparency of a third. Thus a mental edifice is built at an equal distance from the present, from the past, and from fiction—and I find my bearings.

I was very young when the Indochina War broke out. I recall that on two occasions, at an interval of two or three years, we accompanied my uncle to the airport at Le Bourget, where he was to embark on a two-day flight, with stopovers, that would take him to Saigon. At that time the airport was small, even intimate. At his first departure we stayed with him until the moment of his takeoff. In those days I was sensitive to the romanticism of this departure for the Orient. My uncle usually went to Indochina to forget, so I had heard in my entourage; everyone in the family thought that he was seeking a way to die. If that was the case, he didn't find it. For him this departure for Indochina was, I think, in the literal sense, a "new departure." And from my adolescent eyes it was for the hero of my childhood—the man of Casablanca, of submarines, and of the Liberation—a new adventure with an uncertain outcome. He returned from the war once again, always young and always a child at heart, but remarried; for him a new story had begun. In Brittany, during the vacations that followed his return, once or twice he took me on his motorcycle to have a drink among men. Sensing that I was timid, he advised me not to be afraid of girls. He later left the army. He got old and I grew up. But at Le Bourget, before the night flight lifted off once again to carry him far away, I was flushed with the fear of having waved good-bye to him for the last time.

■

At the end of the 1980s I went to Vietnam and to Cambodia. Some places and names reminded me of my uncle. For a first time in my remembrance the history of my family and history as such were briefly conjoined. I would love to have been able to tell him that I followed in his tracks and that I had been thinking of him, but he was no longer there to hear me.

．　．　．　．　．　．

I love the Montparnasse station. Sometimes I walk through it merely for the pleasure of doing so. I love the odor of railway stations. Their smell has surely changed since the era of the steam engine. So, too, have the stations themselves, but when I step along the platforms, my head lowered or nose in the air, alternately, like a dog sniffing its way along a path, I always seem to recover something from the acrid perfume of burning coal and of tar that had formerly imbued them. Montparnasse, furthermore, is the point of departure for the west; it prompts this desire to embark that is quickly extinguished through habit, but born again with the first fresh breeze, with the slightest flicker of daylight in the sky. I browse—*flâne*—about the Montparnasse station as others do on the seashore.

Two streets with magnificently simple names frame the Montparnasse station. They have survived the upheavals out of which, already sometime ago, the new station was born. They are, on one side, the rue du Départ and, on the other, the rue de l'Arrivée. During the war my parents stood in line at four or five o'clock in the morning on the rue du Départ to purchase tickets and reservations for the evening train. They spelled each another, and I sometimes kept company with the one or the other. When the hour of departure arrived, we had to walk for a long time down the platform into the night. The train to Brittany was a night train. We drew and hermetically closed the curtains; before we turned out the lamp and went to sleep, only a little bulb painted blue diffused a semblance of light into the compartment. The train often stopped in the middle of the countryside when bombardments had destroyed the rail beds. It slowly rolled along on the tracks provisionally laid in place. We arrived at our destination only after thirteen or fourteen hours of travel. A peasant whose farm was near the house where my great-aunt from the Parc Saint-Maur had come to live in 1940 awaited us on his buckboard wagon. His name was Glémarec, and he wore a Breton hat with a broad-rimmed visor. We traveled the remaining seven kilometers at the pace of his old horse.

The station where Rick, without Ilsa, finally takes the last train to the south of France was obviously reconstructed in the studio; yet every time I revisit this symbolic place and all its detours and delays at the end of the dramatic flashback that carried us into the recent past of the hero and heroine, its image gets mixed with the memory of the long hours spent during the war years around or inside the Montparnasse station. I lived them as if they were the prerequisite for any escape to the west. Even if the Germans occupied the Breton coast (already in the midst of the exodus they had arrived in Rennes before us!), the countryside and the village discovered in '41 appeared to me to be a haven of liberty and prosperity. This land of abundance, from which every two or three weeks there arrived in Paris packages of butter and bacon drowned in a gravel of rock salt, held in my eyes an existence of a mythic order. The physical ordeal that preceded the embarkation for Brittany (hours standing in line, nocturnal strolls on the windy platform, searches for a good compartment, and the waiting for an often delayed departure) was much like an initiation. I sensed with confusion that it was at once required and normal to undergo the trial of waiting and of travel before arriving in this faraway place that at the time of the exodus we were forever unable to reach.

One evening in Moscow, sometime in the '80s, I felt a strange sensation while looking for my wagon along an endless railway platform. I had just explored Moscow and was en route to Saint Petersburg (Leningrad at the time); all of a sudden I was on the Montparnasse platform forty years before. It must be said that everything conspired to give birth to this fleeting impression: the night, the wind, the odor of coal and smoke, the steam-driven locomotives, and, even more intimately still, the vague anguish that conscience instills in every last-minute traveler, that if they don't hurry, despite the crowd that presses upon them from all sides and the weight of the baggage that slows them down, as in a bad dream, they risk "missing the train." The feeling of urgency once again turned me into a fugitive. Inside the train the warmth and the graciously served tea comforted me, but also prolonged this flashback to childhood: huddled up, as I had been in the closeted shelter of the old-style compartment, I let a few memories float by and dozed off. Upon awakening, in the corridor where the nasal voice of a loudspeaker diffused songs to please the travelers, suddenly (it's not invented nor forgotten either), incongruously, Dalida's voice resounded: "Where have all the flowers gone, Oh where have all the flowers gone, long time passing?"

At the beginning of *Casablanca* a voice-over, based on recent news and with the support of a map, recounts the
exodus of 1940 and the itinerary of those who sought to
embark for America by way of Lisbon through Marseilles,
Oran, and Casablanca. A bold line is drawn on the map
of France from Paris to Marseilles, then a thick dashed
line crosses the Mediterranean and reaches Oran; in a last
shot, the line ends at Casablanca. The simultaneous recall
of the exodus and of Oran sparks my memory and my
imagination. When I was in the military, I twice made the
Marseilles–Oran crossing on a ship run by the Paquet
Company. Three years later, chance had me leave for sub-
Saharan Africa on the same vessel, and I made a stopover
in Casablanca. Furthermore, in Oran I had attended another exodus.

I belong to the generation obsessed by Algeria—the
generation of those who went but who, before departing,
lived in fear of the departure. I spent only a year in Algeria, but for twelve months on end I had tried to imagine
what the tour of duty and the war might be like. I in no
way wished to be part of this war, but I was a prisoner of
the familial mentality that I nonetheless endlessly rejected
and fought against. My uncle, the hero of the Second
World War, and I were on the verge of coming to blows. We
should have been ashamed of ourselves! I was too firmly

in the grip of the family mind-set to envision radical solutions such as desertion—I had neither the courage nor the taste for it—or even cushy solutions, such as exemption on grounds of a chronic nervous condition. I preferred to follow the course of military preparation at the Normale Supérieure that had been, however, required in name only. And so I decided to become an officer. I imagined myself more easily being a disobedient officer, court-martialed and shot by firing squad—yes, I was embellishing a bit—than following orders in silence or getting cuffed by a sadistic corporal. Advanced studies allowed me to buy some time. I was over twenty-six when I left, but it wasn't fear that persuaded me into gaining time—the desire to go and see what was happening was titillating—it was disgust, the certainty of messiness and of stupidity.

The beginning of 1962: when our boat was anchored in the harbor of Oran, waiting to berth in the morning, a few of my buddies and I leaned on the railing for a long time. We made conjectures about the coastline and the entry to the port. It was a strange moment of quiet waiting, much as in westerns before the Indians attack. We were dreamers and, it seems now, both preoccupied and relieved. In any event, that was my state of mind. Oran and its people were subjected to fire and to rampage, but the Algerian War was over.

■

A few weeks later thousands of pieds-noirs waited to board for Spain or France. A vast settlement camp had been improvised. We did our best to manage this new exodus. We weren't wearing the badge of the OAS [the Organisation de l'armée secrète, a clandestine military force that supported French control of Algeria—Trans.] on our breasts because we had been the witness and sometimes the target of its assassination attempts. A certain number of those whom we were trying to help had in all likelihood been partisans. But all these people were poor (the rich were already far away), and the lines that stretched along the platforms in hope of leaving expressed the distress of the entire world.

The magic of names: throughout my childhood I heard about Mers-el-Kébir! In 1940 the English destroyed the French navy at Mers el-Kébir. They were afraid of seeing it rally to the German side. And in fact the French had rejected Churchill's ultimatum to continue the battle or to go to England and disarm. Many died, and Pétain's propaganda machine immediately exploited the disaster. In my family we were sensitive to the humiliation by the Royal Navy, and I seem to have heard cursing about the treacherous English. Twenty-two years later (twenty-two years doesn't amount to much), I took part in the evacuation of French ordnance from the same port of Mers-el-Kébir; but everything went smoothly and calmly, without the slightest problem. The place itself, at least what I had been seeing of it, was unremarkable: warehouses and hangars; the sea, surely, and the roadstead; but the view was far less breathtaking than from the coastal road at Oran. The place did not live up to its name [Mers-el-Kébir is Arabic for "Great Harbor"—Trans.].

Ever since the OAS had been reduced to silence we were stationed at a farm to the west of Oran. Our company was occasionally ordered to lead escort missions. These little sojourns broke the monotony of our lives in the field, and so we readily volunteered to carry them out. I piqued the other second-class lieutenants' jealousy when I was designated to escort a convoy departing from Sidi Bel Abbès. Sidi Bel Abbès, another mythic name. But this time something of the myth was encrusted in it, even if I indeed happened to undo its decorum. Upon arriving at the barracks of the Foreign Legion, I had the impression of landing in a '30s film, and I was soon even more disoriented in that strange place when I met one of my fellow students from the officers' program at the Normale Supérieure. He was a specialist in Latin philology who commanded a squad of legionnaires while working on his thesis. He lived in luxury and had a room of his own. He showed me all the sights. I took a glimpse at the large dining hall. He offered me a glass of wine in the officers' mess, where conscripts employed to serve them performed their tasks impeccably. I was deeply impressed. In all honesty, I felt myself to be a bumpkin. He explained to me that legionnaires were the easiest to command: they were so conditioned to obey that for the superiors it quickly became a habit to impose orders upon them. I took off for Oran with my column of trucks. In the evening, getting back to the farm, I had the comforting feeling of returning to my family, a modest family, yes, but an engaging one too.

．　．　．　．　．　．

My mother was walking with difficulty those last days but, impenitent Parisian that she was, she would never forgo her daily strolls. She knew the network of bus lines like the palm of her hand and plotted her course so that she would do only a section of the first half or return on foot before her energies began to flag. The perimeter of her Parisian domain became progressively restricted, but she never refused to go shopping at the supermarket on the rue Monge or at the open-air market at the place Maubert, nor to walk as far as the Hôtel de Ville in one direction, nor to the Bon Marché in the other when she felt steady on her feet. Along the way, while waiting for the ultimate exodus to Brittany, whose imminence she foresaw, she never stopped going all about the Paris that for us had been that of the Liberation.

From the Liberation I retain a memory map of this intimate Paris that in my eyes has remained the heart of the city. In '45, in front of the Hôtel Lutetia, which had been occupied by the German senior officers during the war, I saw deportees, still dressed in striped clothing, climb down from the trucks that had delivered them there. The war was over. A few months earlier, on the place Maubert, near where we were living, sheltered by the half-closed shutters of a window giving onto the street, I had seen some FFI [Forces françaises de l'intérieur, the French army of the Resistance —Trans.] set German motorcyclists on fire at the corner of the rue de la Montagne-Sainte-Geneviève. In the half hour that followed, some Tiger tanks were visible on the hill by the Cardinal Lemoine subway station, but they did not dare to venture farther. In reprisal they shot a salvo of artillery into the row of buildings on the rue Monge. All the windows were shattered. And then, the next day or the day after, the Second Defensive Battalion passed by under our windows to encamp at the Jardin des Plantes. Today I can still see the wine merchant below us, his arms wrapped around a load of bottles, making his way through the crowd and tendering his offerings to the smiling young men seated on the turrets of their tanks.

Along with my parents, a couple of their friends, and tens of thousands of Parisians, I went to welcome de Gaulle on the square in front of Notre-Dame. I thought I was going die smothered under the crazed crowd when some snipers fired a volley of shots. My father succeeded in tossing me up on his shoulders as best he could. The streets by which we went home, running as we were from one doorway to the next (there were no entry codes and so shelter could be sought everywhere), have today become luxurious thoroughfares in which, at every floor, exposed wooden beams can be seen above antique furnishings. But at that time these were simply poor and dirty streets. We prudently initiated ourselves into what was not yet called urban guerrilla warfare. I recall admiring the chic composure of an American soldier who raised his head to check the rooftops as he kept chewing his gum. The barrel of his submachine gun was smoking; he had just used it, but he was as calm and relaxed as an inquisitive tourist. My mother and her friend had lost their summer dresses in the midst of the battle, and I think that I was amused to see two dignified ladies in their slips running about the street of the Maubert quarter. That became the subject of many conversations in our home.

What would have become of Ilsa and Rick after the war? Even if the film were not fiction, the question would be meaningless. If it is inconceivable in fiction to imagine a sequel to *Casablanca,* it is because in life it is impossible to regress to the past. There is no going back. It is the "River of No Return" that inspires the title of Otto Preminger's film and the melody that Marilyn sings. In Casablanca during the war, Rick and Ilsa's story was open-ended and possible. After the war it's too late. That is what the words of "As Time Goes By" are saying. In truth, they state everything and the opposite: to some that everything is always possible; to others that their turn is done. But the music hardly needs words to say that. Popular melodies are generous, always on hand, always welcoming. It is only that they don't mean the same thing for everyone; nor do they appeal to every generation. Between the false melancholy of those who know that everything can begin and the true sadness of those who believe life is finished, there is the ambiguous space of the melody without words, of three musical notes that play on desire and regret, the desire of regret and the regret of desire. We can imagine that in 1945 Ilsa and Rick would have still been young, that they could have known other adventures, but then, precisely, that would have been another story. There is no sequel to *Casablanca*.

There is a sequel to memories, and that is what makes managing them so delicate. The film of memory is always included in a longer film, the film of life that inflects its meaning because the gaze of he or she who is at once the character, actor, and author always changes. In his book of memories, *The Narrow Waters (Les eaux étroites)*, Julien Gracq meticulously describes the walks he often followed in his early youth along the Èvre, a small tributary of the Loire, and he ends by explaining why he really no longer wishes to take them anymore. For the magic of this excursion was indebted not only to the beauty of the place, which probably is still intact, but also to desire, to the "young blood" of the person strolling along the riverbank who was "turned toward the future." The advent of an older age invalidates this perspective. Any return to the site of an initial dream is forcibly deceptive, as Proust knew through experience, because he imposes the ordeal of an impossible return on himself—this "self" that has moved about and no longer considers time from the same point of view.

I'll let some time go by. I'll wait until next fall.

And I'll leave. I'll go from the Montparnasse station. I'll take the western route. After a few hours I'll be once again on the square in front of the station at Quimperlé, where I haven't set my feet in years. It will not have changed: two bistros, a restaurant, a few gray and sad facades under an autumn rain—a landscape that I know by heart and that formerly made me shudder when my grandparents, who had moved to Brittany in 1950, came to get me during the Christmas holidays or at Easter. Under a light rain I'll find myself suddenly plunged into the depths of depressions of times past. I'll rent a car. The next day, sunshine bursting through the clouds will make the granite walls and camellias sparkle with light, awakening in me the desire to go on to the sea, perhaps, over the wet roads. A wispy sky will extend over the fields like a memory. I'll go to lay flowers on my mother's grave.

I will take the train back in the early afternoon. I will be in Paris again in the evening. I'll harbor the feeling of having been gone for a long time. I will browse around the Latin Quarter for a while and then, when the hour comes, I'll quicken my pace. Going by the Lycée Fénelon, I'll hasten to get to the obscure room where I always feel at home because, endlessly awaiting me, faithful to their post, imperturbable, eternal, will be everyone with whom I've traveled for more than a half century and toward whom I instinctively rush ahead, in evenings of happiness or sadness, sure of their fidelity, of their youth and of mine.

PARIS

Ma

Séine

A WRITER AND HIS MOVIE

Tom Conley

Marc Augé's *Casablanca* counts among a rare number of books that weave the foibles and fortunes of personal and collective memory through a movie. His short essay makes stunningly clear that what we recall as memorable events in our lives are riddled with cinema. Rummaging under our rafters of remembrance, we discover that our earliest impressions are conflated with the films of our childhood. It would be welcome to wager that critics, film scholars, and historians are driven by deeply embedded relations with movies that have marked them, consciously or unconsciously, from their tender years. It would be a safe bet, too, to claim that scholarship produced in the name of film studies is based on a masked law by which a viewer's relation with a film often remains tacit, implied, or, to the inverse, obsessive. A film can be such a force fueling our imagination that were we to reveal our identification with it, we would fear revealing too much of ourselves. Or when extensive critical energies are dedicated to a film, its director, its context, and its history of production or reception, the analysis is built around a *secret* that motivates its labor.

In *Casablanca* Augé takes up these unspoken or nagging relations with film. He chooses Michael Curtiz's film of the same name (1942), a classic that he first saw in 1947, in order to reflect on memory. The result might be called an autobiographical poem. He builds on many of his other works in which the emerging "I" of the writer is synonymous with the anthropologist's gaze that balances attraction to his subject in maintaining a sense of objective focus. An autobiographical "pact" between the writer and his topics, he argues, is based on active and varied relations with the "other" or "others" in the philosophical tradition of alterity that reaches back to the existential (or "prestructural") writings of Claude Lévi-Strauss.[1] The other can be any of a number of native informants who welcome and thwart the ethnologist who queries them in search of rules of kinship. The other can be a familiar object and space, such as a subway station, a railroad platform, a country house, or the interior of a car. In this study Augé shows that they can include—here is one of the essay's enduring innovations—a unique movie that cuts through an individual's ways of living and maintains active relations with the past and present. *Casablanca* becomes a memory machine by which he releases and sorts through volleys of early impressions. With it he sharpens the contours of faint remembrances in order to make them "work with" collective images that tie the individual's past to that of history itself.

On a cursory view, Michael Curtiz's film can be taken to be a catalyst. The film is much like that gram of black-powdered manganese dioxide (we recall from our chemistry classes of long ago) that we mixed in a test tube with a greater quantity of potassium chlorate, which we then put over the flame of a Bunsen burner to release oxygen, which we were told was the medium of life itself. The movie also becomes a point of reference, much like a place-name on a mental map that helps situate an individual in a greater space and time. The images that the author recalls (and reconsiders when he sees it over and over again) allow him to navigate through his past. Film offers (over the costly and often brain-scrambling effects of psychoanalysis) an advantage of perspective. The viewer can return to an "old movie" to locate shifts in attitude and vision because the film remains a template of experience.[2] When seen at different intervals over time, the film allows its viewer to account for the fortunes of identification. When he reaches "a certain age," the viewer—Augé writes for one and for all—looks back over formative films to apprehend the nature of biological and historical transformation. A case in point for a male adult, perhaps a baby boomer, who looks again at *Duck Soup* (1933) or *The Horn Blows at Midnight* (1945): with these two films recalled from childhood or adolescence, he (more likely than she) observes a sea change when Margaret Dumont, a rich wench and proverbial battle-ax, suddenly exudes seductive attraction. Her song charms and her smile radiates. We have changed, and so has our relation with an actor we have finally grown to appreciate.

Along a path of inquiry unlike that of formal inquiry, Augé lets *Casablanca* mesh with the most difficult, indeed traumatizing moments of a collective and national past to that of a French child, no doubt of a middle-class background, with familial ties to the military, growing into a world on the eve of war. As in some of his other works of similar facture—slim, written in a teasingly clear, Cartesian style of autobiography; sustained by anthropological method; peppered with allusions to literature; based on training in both empirical and theoretical traditions; built on clinically "originary scenes"—the book is about goings and comings. The author *goes* to the movies in the Latin Quarter. Before the screen and upon reflection, after *leaving* the theater, he recalls embarkations and departures—*débarquements*—of different scale and proportion, from before the entry of France into World War II up to its retreat from Indochina and defeat in Algeria. His own departures are at play in the fabled exodus with his family in 1940. New and other events, many unknown to his loyal readers, make their way into the account by virtue of what *Casablanca* happens to catalyze.

The mix of things familiar and strange is cause for abandonment of the time-held categories, common to autobiographical theory and to the art of the novel, of degrees of reliability, of veracity, or of picaresque irony. It matters little if the memories are true or false. *Casablanca* hardly plays hide-and-seek, either with its historical background or with the vagaries of autobiography. The writing draws a tenuous line, at times dashed and at others dotted, between confession, "secondary elaboration" (à la Freud), Proustian recall (*In Search of Lost Time* is cited and almost mimed, notably in his ravishment at the sight of poppies waving in a field of wheat), historical reminders (in view of the major dates and events from the prewar through the postwar years), and, best of all, in its avowed confusions (where memories of film cannot be dissociated from formative events). Images from *Casablanca* and other movies constantly flicker through the words, so much so that their presence offsets some of the traumatizing elements of the context of the summer of 1940 and the Occupation that followed.

At first glance one of the paradoxically unsettling effects of the study is found where trauma is treated only obliquely. Little sense of loss or of guilt is passed on to the reader from a writer using autobiography to settle accounts with captors or torturers. The personages in the memoir, *ni victimes ni bourreaux*, neither victims nor hangmen, appear merely to be French citizens living around the rue Monge when the Germans roll across France and march into Paris. They very much resemble the countless individuals shown in his study of Roger-Viollet's collection of photographs of everyday Parisian life in the 1930s in which he wonders about the thoughts that people, shown in open-air markets or on strolls in the city, might (or might not) have had about the horrible future just before them.[3] A narrative of the agonies these civilians or soldiers or civilian victims of the war underwent is partial.[4] Augé is perhaps continuing to draw a line of inquiry begun in *La traversée du Luxembourg*, a book he subtitled "an ethno-novel of a French day considered from the angle of the mores of theory and of happiness."[5] In both studies he inquires of the pleasure that remembrance can afford, especially those moments for which we can be thankful to be alive. The passage of time allows him to jog along the memory lanes of the early years of his home and, as *La traversée, across* a movie whose history constitutes an emblematic frame. He would "prefer not to" rehearse matters of good and bad faith or redraw dividing lines between the partisans of Vichy and those of the Resistance.

Yet, now and again, excruciating reminders come forward. Twice the author is reminded by the cries of pigs being slaughtered in the street, whose shrieks resemble those of babies.[6] Much of the war is shown, as in film noir, sotto voce or as what elsewhere he has called an "immaterial and diffuse menace."[7] The most disquieting instance of *Casablanca* is found in the two epigraphs. The first is from Robert Desnos and the other from Augé, in which he notes that the book is one montage among many. Desnos, however, seems to give the lie to the author's painstaking labor of reminiscence: "I try to remember, but I have neither the power nor perhaps the desire."[8] An acclaimed surrealist poet, Desnos was known for trying to remember his own poem "J'ai tant rêvé de toi" (I have dreamed so much of you) (first published in 1936, in *Corps et biens*)—a moving love poem known for its axial image, "O balances sentimentales" (oh sentimental scales)—when he lay dying, on June 8, 1945, in the Theresienstadt concentration camp, in Czechoslovakia, which the Germans had abandoned one month before, just prior to the arrival of the Allied troops. Desnos had been a member of the French Resistance before the Gestapo arrested him in February 1944. He was sent to Buchenwald and soon after found himself in constant exodus, transported from one camp to another, before he died with the poem of his youth on the tip of his tongue.

Augé acknowledges that next to many of his coequals his fate was charmed. Much of *Casablanca* moves along the edge of a literature of remembrance among a generation of either very young survivors of the war or those who were born just before, during, or at its end. In a brilliant study of this intermediate canon Susan Suleiman shows these works mix veracious report with obsessive phantasms.[9] Sometimes the authors evince a desire to have been active participants in the conflicts; to seek a way to share the suffering; or, indirectly, to express contrition and guilt, because they were nurtured out of the nightmare, about living in the shadow of those who were exterminated. At times the reiterated remembrance of the events puts them into sharp relief, and at others it blurs them. When they are fashioned in experimental form, they are shaped (like Georges Perec's *La disparition*) around elements that cannot be recalled, or even written, whether by fate or by design (like the letter *e* in Perec's novel).

Unlike the authors and filmmakers whom Suleiman studies, Augé writes neither from the camps nor in direct view of them. Yet, as an ethnologist who witnessed the utter and implacable destruction of indigenous cultures under colonial rule (first in Ivory Coast),[10] Augé is well aware of the most destructive designs the world has seen enacted upon itself. Having been under the tutelage of Claude Lévi-Strauss, he is more than familiar with the colonial heritage. To this day, from *Tristes tropiques,* Lévi-Strauss reminds his students and readers about the holocaust of South America: how Spanish and Portuguese ships fired rags infected with syphilis into the populations of South America and soon decimated them; how the imposition of Christianity and commercial exploitation amounted to enslavement; how the growth of Brazilian cities gave birth to widespread poverty and destitution.[11] Of a similar outlook, in what Georges Balandier called "the colonial situation,"[12] from the beginning of his career Augé has been active witness to the work of Christian missionaries in African communities who erase the bonds of collective identity that paganism had assured for them.[13]

From the standpoint of Susan Suleiman's spirited and informed reading of Augé's *Les formes de l'oubli,*[14] some designs of *Casablanca* can be discerned with greater clarity. In her concluding chapter Suleiman invokes Augé to set forward the delicate issue of amnesia and amnesty in France in the postwar years. Prior to engaging his book she sums up the styles of the writers of her chosen canon. By means of preterition, the way by which they can "say without saying," her authors bring trauma forward through "strategies of suspension, postponement, digression, juxtaposition, and metacommentary." This approach allows them to fashion an "experimental writing about childhood trauma, in particular the experience of childhood loss."[15] Appeal is made to Freud's *Ichspaltung*, the concept of the divided ego, developed in his classic essay on fetishism (1927) and in another, penned on the eve of the Second World War (prior to the moment Freud, embarking for London, left his home in Vienna), "Splitting of the Ego in the Defensive Process" (1938). The latter essay, distinguishing neurosis from psychosis, reveals that among writers, coping with their past fetishism is of a piece with preterition. Often associated with the creative drive, it is a structure of "simultaneous denial and affirmation of reality."[16] The writer selects fetishes in order simultaneously to recognize and to deny childhood trauma. Preterition becomes the mode by which the writer works "out of" and "through" the past or, better, "with" the memories of events that took place within the frame of the war years. Artists have the advantage of shaping their media to retrieve, refashion, and reformulate the matter of memory for ends that are both creative and therapeutic.

Prior to invoking Augé in the opening paragraph of her conclusion, Suleiman notes that they conjoin "experiment with existence" to yield "structures of approach and avoidance, of event and erasure."[17] His "short but profound book *Les formes de l'oubli*"[18] is built on the observation that memory cannot be done without oblivion, and that as he describes them, memories can be likened to the contours of a shore that the sea, a process of forgetting, continually reshapes. Written with a coy Erasmian irony, "in praise of forgetting," Augé complicates what is generally inferred by the "duty to remember." Suleiman rightly inquires of the ideology of forgetting by observing how, after the war, certain kinds of oblivion are based on a will to forgive those responsible for the Holocaust. How and where forgetting can turn into a "reprehensible amnesia" in view of a far more noble *act* (in the Sartrean idiolect, that stands in contrast to the velleity of a *gesture*) of forgiveness bears on the postwar issue of amnesty. In France after 1945, amnesty amounted to a forced forgetting, to a sanctioned eradication of hauntingly difficult memories. Here, Suleiman notes that Augé's call in *Les formes de l'oubli* for a "'duty to forget' in order not to repeat the past" seems problematic.[19] Which, in a keen turn, she studies in the context of the South African Truth and Reconciliation Commission, the council that granted limited amnesty to groups and individuals who violated human rights in exchange for forthright accounts of their actions. Amnesty was aimed at fostering *disclosure* and not oblivion. If there is a duty to forget, argued the commission, it cannot be tied to the repressive dictates of amnesty that France sanctioned. The issue was and is to "forgive without effacing the debt owed to the dead, for both individuals and societies that have experienced—as all too many individuals have in the past century—acts of collective violence and hatred."[20]

In *Casablanca* Augé undertakes to *work with* and revise some of the reflections in *Les formes de l'oubli*. Of Augé's writings, this work implies that all of us have a "duty to remember." A "user's guide" for journeys into our remote past, it conjoins singular wartime memories—his alone—with others, collective, that through cinema splinter into partially historical, partially personal forms of memory. Germans are called Germans, perhaps in order not to confuse the human beings who were at war with the associations summoned by the horrible word "Nazi" and the gammadion, its repulsive emblem. The "other" that the child had seen is recalled through the lens of the anthropologist that he has since become. Augé notes abundantly how his family, having a long-standing affiliation with the French military, shifted from a Maginot mentality in the prewar years (a mentality that might have held its remembrance of the "Great War" in high esteem) to admire the Resistance. He shows how the family that lived under the Occupation nonetheless committed itself to the cause of liberation from the nation's misbegotten wars in Indochina and Algeria. He is quick to recall, too, that he alienated himself from his family when he took a dissident view of those conflicts.

For what concerns the labors of memory and residual trauma, *Casablanca* offers comparison to Sarah Kofman's childhood memoir, *Rue Ordener, Rue Labat.* Kofman's short work, of similar length and also built as a montage, begins with the account of her pilfering from her mother's purse an old fountain pen that had belonged to her dead father. She gazes on the fetish object in order, it appears, to engage the writing of the twenty-odd "scenes" that follow. The author presents the childhood years through the filter of an analysis confirming Melanie Klein's hypotheses about psychogenesis. The "bad" biological mother, a Jew who weathers the loss of her husband (the author's father), a rabbi who gave himself over to the Nazis in a first *rafale* of the Final Solution, has a "good" Christian counterpart (named

Mémé), who hides and saves the girl during the Occupation. Following a violent confrontation between the real and the surrogate mother, the daughter finds herself both devastated and relieved when she is forced to return to her maternal home. Much like Augé's *Casablanca,* which ends at the author's mother's grave, *Rue Ordener, Rue Labat* concludes with the author's remembrance of how a Christian priest, speaking at Mémé's funeral, spoke of the selfless deeds of a woman "who saved a little Jewish girl during the war."

Just prior to that moment Kofman inserts two photographic reminiscences. The first, from Leonardo da Vinci's painting *Saint Anne with the Virgin,* one of the works treated in Freud's great study (1907) of the way memory constantly rewrites and revises the past, is the very image Kofman had chosen to put on the cover of her first book, *L'enfance de l'art* (The Childhood of Art). The other is taken from what the author felt to be a traumatizing moment in one of her favorite films, *The Lady Vanishes* (1938). The next-to-last film that Alfred Hitchcock directed in England before he emigrated to the United States (roughly synchronous with Freud's embarkation for London), the feature turns on the moment when Iris (Margaret Lockwood), the half-dazed protagonist who has bonded with a warm, maternal, and *good* British governess (Dame May Whitty), awakens from her sleep to discover the chilling gaze of a cold, frightening, and *bad* woman in the seat of the governess. Iris becomes almost hysterically committed to find the missing lady. She ultimately succeeds and brings the film to its famously happy end in London. But for Kofman the two figures, the good governess and her bad counterpart, constitute an almost perfect analogue for what in the context of her autobiography was the dilemma of being raised between two mothers.

The outcome of the relation that the film memory bore with the author was not so happy. Shortly after completing *Rue Ordener, Rue Labat,* Kofman took her own life. Hitchcock's film had surely been a memory prod, but also an agent that reconfirmed a sense of trauma and helplessness. It was taken in the design of an allegory out of which, perhaps for reasons of guilt and untold suffering, the author found no issue. *The Lady Vanishes* fits into the autobiography such that, unlike *Casablanca* in Augé's essay, it does not catalyze other memories or allow the author to divagate and to wander about the past. Augé's recall of his film has some parallels with what Kofman did with Hitchcock's thriller, but it is used less to figure in a fearful symmetry than to allow remembrance to dilate and to bring breath and force to the inventions we make of ourselves with our past and the movies that make that past what it is.

The memories on which Augé's *Casablanca* builds and varies attest to the virtue of film as a fetish and a vitally intermediate or "transitive" object that allows him to cope with difficult material. Augé reiterates or "returns" over and again to scenes that change by virtue of their context. The first sentences of *Un ethnologue dans le métro* begin in 1940, at the Maubert-Mutualité station, "upon return from the exodus."[21] A nagging reminiscence inaugurates his inquiry into the underground rapid transit when he recalls that by the Maubert-Mutualité entry to the subway stop the "hurried silhouette" of a German "wearing a gray soldier's cap passes by."[22] The fleeting impression gives way to the exodus, described sketchily as an itinerary that the invading Germans were endlessly interrupting and that caused the family constantly to reroute itself and revise its plans. He remembers an airplane buzzing over the flatlands of the Sarthe that prompted fear and curiosity. "It was a blurred absence, an abstraction forever on the point of materializing."[23] In *Domaines et châteaux,* similar memories of the exodus recur:

> The exodus: others have known it to be more dramatic. But however uncertain may be the memories I believe that what I retain of it has greatly impressed my memory. The road we had to take by night after several days of calm in the flatlands of Champagné were for me only a long and chaotic sleep punctuated by fugitive awakenings—halts marked by the flash of searchlights and the hurried words policemen exchanged in loud voices. The Loire: the word constantly comes back. The Loire, border, that we were continually harboring doubts about crossing ... The Pyrenees (ten days must have passed): I awaken in a sunlit bedroom; for the first time in my life I see mountains. The retreat is over. We've arrived. Soon we'll go back home.[24]

These events are noted to have taken place in 1940, seven years before *Casablanca* was shown in French theaters.[25] In that film we vividly recall the map of France superimposed over (recently taken) stock shots of throngs of people in exodus, en route from Paris to Marseilles and from Marseilles across the Mediterranean, to the shores of North Africa. In its last shot the unforgettable montage brings the line to meet the bold dot marking "Casablanca."[26]

In Augé's more recent account—no doubt because Curtiz's film interferes with his recall—the memories gain greater relief and a sharper edge. They move backward, to the prewar years, and forward, to the Liberation. What he describes is unique, of his experience alone, but also of collective access. But thanks to the prod of *Casablanca* and to the unique reflective style of Augé's writing, they are ours as well. What he retrieves from the last days of Paris before the Liberation correlates with contemporary newsreels and photographic histories of World War II: after Resistance fighters have immolated two German motorcyclists, Tiger tanks stationed at the rue Cardinal Lemoine subway station fire in reprisal upon the buildings along the rue Monge; or his recollection of a gritty, unshaven but nonchalant, gumchewing American soldier, his smoking submachine gun in hand, looking at the rooftops where he might have just gunned down a sniper. The recollections accumulating here and in Augé's other essays leave the effect, much like that of a New Wave film, of enticing the viewer to follow an ever-bifurcating path through images, both past and present, and to employ those images as reminders of our own relations (and those of our kin) with events that shape history. The reiterations confirm Augé's argument that a duty to forget and a duty to remember are one and the same. From one book to the next the process develops further, the plot thickens, the montage extends.[27]

Obviously the beauty and pleasure of *Casablanca* are felt in the way Augé writes of these inextricably mixed memories and images. Only a scholar of classical training could look at the romance of separation at the end of *Casablanca* through the double lens of Corneille's *Tite et Bérénice* and Racine's historical complement and rival, *Bérénice*. The tragedy that duty imposes on love had been a French schoolchild's lesson. The two playwrights wove their plots about the Roman emperor Titus, destroyer of Jerusalem, who was unable to marry Berenice because of Roman anti-Semitism. Memories from the canon put the drama of Rick (Humphrey Bogart) and Ilsa (Ingrid Bergman) into a perspective that every French schoolchild knew by heart. And the closer one reads, the richer are the rewards. On the last page the luminous paragraphs describing sunshine striking camellias and wet granite in Brittany find analogues in Joseph L. Mankiewicz's *The Barefoot Contessa* (1954), a film based on a long and even traumatizing flashback.[28] The Breton landscape is mixed with reminders of a poem by Victor Hugo, also known to every French schoolchild, announcing the visit he will make to his daughter's (Léopoldine's) grave: "Demain, dès l'aube, à l'heure où blanchit la campagne, je partirai" (Tomorrow, as of dawn, at the hour the countryside brightens, I'll leave).

The oblique meaning of this line of *poésie pure* (pure poetry)[29] hooks into the ubiquitous departures and embarkations in which the first shots of *Casablanca* are threaded through Augé's memories of his early and later years, along with indirect reference to his other works in which Arthur Rimbaud is present. Reminders of "Le bateau ivre" are found where the speaker embarks on adventures of the senses through a play of language and sensation. Rimbaud is the absent prodigal son in Augé's first official novel, *La mère d'Arthur*.[30] And at the end of *Un ethnologue dans le metro,* the reader finds Augé once again *embarking,* through literature, when he expands on the pure poetry of a warning stenciled on the portals of the Parisian subway: "Le train ne peut partir que les portes fermées" (the train can leave only with the doors closed). Taught to him by a teacher who fetishized French prosody, this "absolutely perfect" and ready-made alexandrine leads to a reflection on the existential anguish Pascal generates in the *Pensées*. In the same breath he notes that the high school teacher who informed him of classical verse in the subway also explicated *nous sommes embarqués* (we've embarked), the one-liner that from one point of view anticipates an exodus while, from another (memory), helps the author retrieve and sort through much of his formative education.

Cinematic and literary connections become further emplotted in the implicit spatial and historical geography of the book. Paris, to be sure, is one axis. The provinces, as they have been alternately immortalized and forgotten, are another. When in his early childhood Augé reaches the Landes forest southwest of Bordeaux, he enters into the sacred world of François Mauriac, author of troubled novels (whose godlike point of view Sartre famously called into question) that make the dark and thick pine forests the object of his uncanny descriptive powers. (In 1953 Georges Franju had in fact directed an outstanding adaptation, a feature of a style and texture synchronous with *Les jeux interdits*, the film with which Augé mixes his own reminiscences.) The seductive and oneiric atmosphere—French literature and film are said to be about atmosphere—of Gérard de Nerval's Île-de-France is felt through words grafted from "El Desdichado" in the description of Augé's fabled uncle, a submarine commander in the French navy at the beginning of the war. "If the name 'Casablanca' still shines in my eyes with a special aura, it owes a debt to the memory of the dark and handsome hero returning from the war to encounter death, the hero with a tumultuous past, the inconsolable widower." The uncle is portrayed with the words of one of the most beauteous and even chilling sonnets in the history of French poetry: "Je suis le ténébreux, —le veuf, —l'inconsolé, / Le prince d'Aquitaine à la tour abolie" (I am the melancholy one, the widower, the disconsolate, / The prince of Aquitaine in the abolished tower). Nerval's dark hero, drawn in part from the image of the hanged man on the tarot card, is altered to describe the hero who emerged—literally and metaphorically—out of a deep and murky past.

The description that moves French readers in one way captures their American counterparts in another. If the latter fail to detect the displacement of Nerval's *Chimères* into the verbal texture, they quickly discover correlative images of troubled commanders who, instead of casting their gaze from an "abolished tower," look through binoculars from the conning towers of their submarines. When Augé reconstructs his uncle's feat of setting his vessel on the ocean floor, then releasing drafts of engine oil and flotsam to fool the enemy above into believing that they had sunk the submarine, the man becomes (at least for amateurs of the extraordinary genre of the "submarine movie") a double of Clark Gable and Burt Lancaster in *Run Silent, Run Deep*. Networks of poetic and filmic figures mesh in ways that the writer-directors of the New Wave developed when they wove much of French literature into their cinemas. Augé works along a similar line in calling for a process of recollection that is forever inventing itself through its myriad relations with words and images.

We tend to forget when we see the place-name "Casablanca" that the word can mean "white house." In Augé's psychogeography the city is a real place tied to the history of his family. The name figures, too, in much of the corresponding synesthesia in the volume. "On parlait beaucoup de Casablanca, chez moi, pendant la guerre" (At home they spoke to me a lot about Casablanca during the war). The words—at least in the decasyllable constituting the sentence proper—cue on a drama of space, name, and place: what does it mean to be "at home"? Incised in the name of the city of whitewashed walls, an implied "home" causes it to allude to the constant displacement of the author's family. Augé seems—but only seems—to draw on Freud's "Uncanny" (1919), a work of partial reminiscence also born of war and death. Augé's French family is established, it coheres, and it has strong lines of affiliation. Its members remain in close contact with one another, but it is carried off in a movement of exodus that goes both inward and outward.

Hence the importance of Augé's final westward journey, taken from the Montparnasse station, aiming toward "the end of the earth," the Finistère. It ends within the confines of what becomes, in the Proustian sentence that clinches the essay, an homage to the family and to a sense of *chez moi* that extends back to the movie houses of the Latin Quarter and forward, to a countless number of kin, friends, and colleagues who have made his life what it is: a genial shift from a nuclear (bourgeois) core to a deeper and richer extended family and, at the same time, a creative way of rethinking the kinship structures that inform his field of inquiry. Because *chez moi* is located in the movie theater of the fifth and six arrondissements, and because the first of kin in the book are the cashier and the *ouvreuse* at the Action Christine, "home" is tied to the vital *solitude* of the experience of film. *Casablanca* and its presence in the family signal that to be who one "is" and to live in a moderate degree of sanity depend on a careful and conscientious negotiation of familiarity and alterity.

That very life-giving negotiation is the topic Augé studies from the standpoint of anthropology in *Le métier d'anthropologue*.[31] Its conclusions go well with the meanderings of *Casablanca*. In *Le métier* he draws from Claude Lévi-Strauss, who argues in his *Introduction to the Work of Marcel Mauss,* in Augé's words, that "an individual experiences his or her own identity solely through relations with others," but that "those whom we call sane of mind," because they consented to live in a world defined only by self and other, are indeed those who are insane *(insensés)*. They are those who summon the meaning of *sense,* "not a metaphysical or transcending sense, but a social relation itself insofar as it is represented and instituted."[32] They are *insensed* because they encounter, like all of us, chance and the unknown, two elements that have no "place" in a closed system. Lévi-Strauss remarked that in every society a field of tension opens when "sense, understood as a sum of relations that can be imagined, and liberty, defined as the space given to individual initiatives," are in play.[33] In his conclusion, titled "writing" *(l'écriture),* Augé asks why great anthropologists in France have succumbed to the temptations of writing: probably "because the supplementary degree of exteriority and liberty they accorded themselves *in their own style* allows them to relate their experience, to discern the areas of shadow and uncertainty, that no inquiry ever succeeds in completely dissipating, but also, inversely, in going beyond strict limits in order to broaden the field of reflection. That is what it is to be outside and in, at a distance and a participant."[34] That, too, is what it is to read and to write from *Casablanca:* from an essay that also succumbs to the temptation to write and that recovers the dark and uncertain areas of memories that inspire the will to write.[35]

Readers of *Casablanca,* some no doubt of the generation of the translator (born December 7, 1943, which in our family we called a second day of infamy), who admire the intellectual, literary, and cinematic heritage of France, obtain added pleasure in observing how Augé finds solace and sanctuary in the little movie houses of the Latin Quarter. For years it has been an unspoken truth that to see and learn about American cinema, the place to be is Paris. Films rarely projected outside film studies departments in North America (of late, Monte Hellman's *Two-Lane Blacktop*), that are practically censored (Sam Fuller's *Shock Corridor,* hardly a candidate for American Movie Classics), or that are never seen in the land of the multiplex are daily fare in Paris. But one difference is that the student of French who grows into the language and civilization from a monolingual origin endlessly encounters "mirror stages" of untold chagrin when learning to speak and write the idiom that the natives, especially Parisians, are known to fetishize with jealous delight. The "American in Paris" attains bliss in retreating to the Studio Cujas, the Action Christine, or venturing from the boulevard Saint-Michel to the far end of the rue de Babylone, to find the Pagoda, where American films offer both relief from French and outstanding shorthand instruction—a lazy person's Berlitz—in the strips of subtitles. The viewer feels relieved, his or her frustrations assuaged, upon watching the scene in *A Night at the Opera* when Chico and Groucho scroll along the lines of the two copies of a contract at the end of which they discover finally that indeed there is no "sanity clause." The pun finds no written equivalent, no sign of a "Père Noël."

Or when, hunkering down with Jane Russell in an abandoned cabin in Montana while cold winds whistle in *The Tall Men* (a

1955 western often seen in Paris, seldom in North America), a wizened and leathery Clark Gable glances at a rabbit simmering on the fire. He exchanges a glance with the fresh and feisty beauty and looks skyward. Attempting to endear himself to her (and staking his future on the conjugal bliss they will never share), he wryly utters, "Ah, I got nothin' to complain about. A roof over my head. Fire goin' strong . . . solid home cookin' . . . What else could a man want?" The subtitle, in perfect synchrony, deliciously captures the spirit of the moment: "Y'a rien comme de la bonne cuisine bourgeoise." Between one idiom and the other, does the remark apply to the film itself? To our pleasure of seeing old American movies on the Rive Gauche? Or to the effect that movies have always been a *cuisine bourgeoise*? Surely, but as Augé shows, that and much more. Gifted writer that he is, he invites his readers to follow his path, in and out of movies in the Latin Quarter; and to find a means of writing about them objectively, but also in wandering through the folds of memory, capturing force of attraction that forever draws us to the movies.

NOTES

1. In their rich overview of Augé's career, Jean-Paul Colleyn and Jean-Pierre Dozon remark that Lévi-Strauss's *Introduction to the Work of Marcel Mauss* (1950) has remained a point of reference for study of the mobility of ethnic identity. It can be added, too, that in the postwar years Lévi-Strauss's *Tristes tropiques* (Paris: Plon, 1955) was the "ethnologist's breviary" for anyone seeking to mix anthropology with autobiography. See Colleyn and Dozon, "Lieux et non-lieux de Marc Augé," 7–32, in "L'anthropologue et le contemporain: Autour de Marc Augé." Special issue of *L'Homme: Revue Française d'Anthropologie* 185–86

(January–June) (Paris: Editions de l'École en Hautes Études en Sciences Sociales, 2008).

2. These words ought not be taken to impugn psychoanalysis but, rather, to suggest, as Félix Guattari once noted, that cinema is the "poor man's divan." Guattari, "Le divan du pauvre," *Communications* (special issue on psychoanalysis and cinema), no. 23 (1973): 146–58. Some of the scrambling effects of psychoanalysis can be inferred from the fate of Sarah Kofman. See her memoir, discussed in this afterword: *Rue Ordener, Rue Labat,* translated and with an introduction by Ann Smock (Lincoln: University of Nebraska Press, 1996); originally published as *Rue Ordener, Rue Labat* (Paris: Galilée, 1994).

3. Marc Augé, *Paris années trente Roger-Viollet* (Paris: Hazan, 1996).

4. For this reader a benchmark first-person treatment of the experience of hardship and survival in World War II is Sidney Stewart's *Give Us This Day* (1957; New York: Norton, 1999). The author, a prisoner of the Japanese who endured excruciating hardship (and lived to become a practicing psychoanalyst in Paris), underscores the extent to which tenderness and shared faith kept the prisoners alive, especially in horrendous conditions. Some of the most complex accounts of trauma that children experienced in the war and have negotiated by way of writing are taken up in Susan Suleiman, *Crises of Memory and the Second World War* (Cambridge, Mass.: Harvard University Press, 2006).

5. Marc Augé, *La traversée du Luxembourg: Ethno-roman d'une journée française considérée sous l'angle des moeurs de la théorie et du bonheur* (Paris: Hachette, 1985).

6. These episodes have a traumatic analogy in cinema, for no reader can fail to be reminded of *Roma, città aperta* (1945) in which, at a moment of calm (in a local restaurant), a German soldier puts his Luger to the heads of two sheep, pulls the trigger, and, *cut,* the gun blast is matched by the horrified gaze of Marina (Maria Michi), looking on the scene, who does not realize the character of the assassins with whom she is passively collaborating.

7. Marc Augé, *In the Metro,* translated with an introduction and an afterword by Tom Conley (Minneapolis: University of Minnesota Press, 2002), 7; originally published as *Un ethnologue dans le métro* (Paris: Hachette, 1986).

8. Marie-Claire Dumas, ed., *Robert Desnos: Oeuvres* (Paris: Gallimard/Quarto, 1999), 969.

9. Suleiman, *Crises of Memory and the Second World War.*

10. Marc Augé, *Le rivage alladian: Organisation et évoloution des villages alladian (Côte d'Ivoire)* (Paris: Orstrom, 1969).

11. Lévi-Strauss, *Tristes tropiques* (Paris: Plon, 1955) 81–82, 337, 426–28.

12. See Georges Balandier, *Anthropologie politique* (Paris: Presses Universitaires de France, 1979), 201–2 and elsewhere.

13. The demography of the Nambikwara is one of disparition (Lévi-Strauss, *Tristes tropiques,* 337); the impact of capitalism on the Tupi is harrowing (ibid., 422–23). *Tristes tropiques* is equally built on the labor of remembrance. The author arches the account he wrote in the early 1950s over the war and to his experience of Brazil in the prewar years. Two recent studies affirm Augé's observations about how populations are subjected to and controlled by imposed dualism of Judeo-Christian stamp: André Mary studies Pentecostalism and witchcraft in view of Manichaean structures; Mary, "Actualité du paganisme et contemporanéité des prophétismes," in Colleyn and Dozon, "L'anthropologue et le contemporain," 365–86. Paulin Hountondji takes up Augé's work on Christian control of African mental structures; Hountondji, "Une pensée-prépersonnelle: Note sur ethnophilosophie et idéo-logique de Marc Augé," in Colleyn and Dozon, "L'anthropologue et le contemporain," 342–60, especially 356.

14. Marc Augé, *Les formes de l'oubli* (Paris: Payot & Rivages, 1998); translated by Marjolijn de Jager as *Oblivion* (Minneapolis: University of Minnesota Press, 2004).

15. Suleiman, *Crises of Memory and the Second World War,* 208.

16. Ibid., 210.

17. Ibid., 214.

18. Ibid., 215.

19. Ibid., 225.

20. Ibid., 272.

21. Augé, *Un ethnologue dans le métro*, 7; *In the Metro*, 3.

22. Augé, *Un ethnologue dans le métro*, 8; *In the Metro*, 4. Like *Casablanca*, the work can be qualified as a *petit poème en prose*. The hurried silhouette—"la *silhouette* pressée d'un homme au calot gris"—gives way to an uncommon figure of memory that literally rhymes with this image. The subway becomes a memory aid, a memory machine, or a pocket mirror "où viennent se refléter et s'affoler un instant les *alouettes* du passé" (on which are instantly reflected the skylarks of the past).

23. Ibid.

24. Augé, *Domaines et châteaux* (Paris: Seuil, 1989), 98–99.

25. In "The Limitless Potentials and the Potential Limits of Classical Hollywood Cinema," Dana Polan reviews the history of the feature and furnishes a copious bibliography attesting to what Augé mentions in passing. Polan, in *Film Analysis: A Norton Reader,* edited by Jeffrey Geiger and R. L. Rutsky, 362–79 (New York: W. W. Norton, 2005).

26. The sequence that begins from a shot of the globe showing the Pacific Ocean and the eastern shores of Asia ends upon the arrival of a line of itinerary (begun in Paris) at Casablanca. It lasts eighty-three seconds and superimposes maps over newsreel footage to elide history and fiction. Analysis of the beginning and the flashback of the film are taken up in Augé's study and in Tom Conley, *Cartographic Cinema* (Minneapolis: University of Minnesota Press, 2007), 94–99.

27. What of the *colors* of the images? A recent show at the Hôtel de Ville (spring 2008) exhibited the Lumière Brothers' *autochromes* of Paris from the turn of the twentieth century, images from Albert Kahn's *Archives de la planète,* André Zucca's photographic propaganda of everyday life, and snippets from postwar Technicolor movies. Life that

had been generally represented in black and white is shown in color, and with it come unsettling and even traumatizing effects. Jean-Luc Godard notes that the world changed when Georges Stevens became the first photographer to record in 16 mm color stock what the Allies discovered upon entering Auschwitz and Ravensbrück; see Godard's *Histoire(s) du cinéma* (Paris: Gallimard, 1989). He superimposes those images (which Stevens had left in the basement of his home) over the swimming pool sequence (with Elizabeth Taylor and Montgomery Clift) of Stevens's *A Place in the Sun* (1953). He castigates Hollywood (and both the American war and media forces) for failing to own up to its own repressive effects. The digital art of recombination literally reinvents memories and shatters any forced oblivion of the camps. Jacques Rancière offers a close and meticulous reading of the double binds inhering in the way in which film "remembers" the war; Rancière, *La fable cinématographique* (Paris: Seuil, 2001), (217–37).

28. When the translator happened upon those sentences, the beginning and end of *The Barefoot Contessa* (1954) came to mind. The personal delight was soon tempered and confirmed—shown to belong to a community of viewers—when it was noted that Jean Janin, in a careful reading of *Casablanca*, refers to the same sequences: "the last scene of *Casablanca* (the book), entirely written in the indicative future (a sort of flash-forward), cannot go without my recalling the first sequence-shot of Joseph Mankiewicz's *Barefoot Contessa*, and therein resides the 'force of attraction' of cinema." Janin, "Vues de *Casablanca*," in Colleyn and Dozon, "L'anthropologue et le contemporain," 241–52.

29. Alfred Glauser shows how, as Gide noted ("Victor Hugo, hélas") at the time of the Abbé Bremond's debates on poetry that transcends representation, Hugo is the "purest" of French poets. The stake of art in those debates and in the French literary tradition in general imbues Augé's fragmentary quotations that run through the work. See Glauser, *Victor Hugo et la poésie pure* (Paris: Droz, 1959).

30. Marc Augé, *La mère d'Arthur* (Paris: Fayard, 2005).

31. Marc Augé, *Le métier d'anthropoloque: Sens et liberté* (Paris: Galilée, 2006).

32. Ibid., 37–38.

33. Ibid., 39–40.

34. Ibid., emphasis added. In *Le métro revisité,* with practically the same words, Augé reflects on how his study of the metro used Lévi-Strauss's dictum that ethnologists must take an objective distance with respect to themselves at the same time that they enter "as profoundly as possible in the subjectivity of those whom they are observing. It wasn't difficult for me to slip into the habits of the everyday subway rider: I was one; nor into those of the ethnologist: I was that too. I observed myself, directly or through memory, and I had no less difficulty in objectifying myself as in others too, in the subway, riding with their memories, their projects, their emotions, their constraints and their contradictions." Augé, *Le métro revisité* (Paris: Seuil, 2008), 25–26, 26–27.

35. In "Le métier d'écrire," the translator argues that Augé's works cue on what Lévi-Strauss called a *léçon d'écriture* (*Tristes tropiques,* 345–65), a harmonics of inscription in which sound and inscription are simultaneous, much like the play of sight and sound in the medium of cinema. Conley, "Le métier d'écrire," in Colleyn and Dozon, "L'anthropologue et le contemporain," 333–42.

MARC AUGÉ, an anthropologist trained in French universities, has studied and written copiously on North African cultures. He teaches leading seminars at École des Hautes Études en Sciences Sociales in Paris and is author of many books, including *La traversée du Luxembourg, Domaines et châteaux, Non-lieux: Introduction à l'anthropologie de la surmodernité, Un ethnologue dans le métro,* and *Les formes de l'oubli.* The English translations *In the Metro* and *Oblivion* have been published by the University of Minnesota Press.

TOM CONLEY is Lowell Professor of Romance languages and film studies at Harvard University. His publications from the University of Minnesota Press include *Cartographic Cinema* (2007), *Film Hieroglyphs: Ruptures in Classical Cinema* (1991; new edition, 2006), and *The Self-Made Map: Cartographic Writing in Early Modern France* (1996). His translations published by the University of Minnesota Press include *The Fold: Leibniz and the Baroque,* by Gilles Deleuze; *Culture in the Plural* and *The Capture of Speech and Other Political Writings,* by Michel de Certeau; and *In the Metro,* by Marc Augé.